Living on the Edge

Risky Advice from a Senior Millennial

Thomas N. Wisley

WestBow
PRESS®
A DIVISION OF THOMAS NELSON
& ZONDERVAN

WestBow Press books may be ordered through booksellers or by contacting:

WestBow Press
A Division of Thomas Nelson & Zondervan
1663 Liberty Drive
Bloomington, IN 47403
www.westbowpress.com
1 (866) 928-1240

ISBN: 978-1-9736-6656-1 (sc)
ISBN: 978-1-9736-6657-8 (e)

Print information available on the last page.

WestBow Press rev. date: 07/05/2019

CONTENTS

FOREWORD

I hope the title of this book is more of a challenge than a turn-off. I mean, who really wants to listen to the advice of another? Fortunately, there are some who do, at least some who want the input of others who've "been there, done that." It's to those people I'm writing.

So, what do I mean by "risky advice?"

The Cambridge Dictionary defines advice as "an opinion that someone offers about what you should do or how you should act in a particular situation." The word "risky" suggests danger, fraught with the threat of failure or loss. Putting these words together I hope to convey the idea that the danger of failure or loss might ensue if you follow any advice I might give. I say this "tongue in cheek." I find many who seek it.

A FEW
DISCLAIMERS

First, there are good books that delve deeply and strategically into the Millennial worldview. I've attempted to summarize some of those sources so that I can focus primarily on the "advice" section. In that regard I don't profess to be an expert on the nuances of Millennial worldview.

Second the reason I'm writing with Millennials in mind is because I like this generation. I'll say more about that below but want to clarify some of the bad press the Millennial generation has gotten. However I distinguish between Millennials who share the Christian or Biblical worldview from a non-Christian or secular worldview.

Third, I'm accustomed to this age group. I like their unique generational characteristics; their freshness, aliveness, alert minds and eagerness for new experiences.

Fourth I've observed that many Christian Millennials are not only open to mentorship but also desirous for it. Much of the content for this book has been gleaned from my interactions with Christian Millennials both at the Church where my wife and I attend and in private mentoring sessions we have had with Christian Millennials.

Finally, my cross-cultural training in culture and communications contribute heavily to my interest in cultural differences, including generational differences. Insights from cultural Anthropology and Intercultural Communications help me to understand people from within their cultural world. I learn about their worldview, their values, language, social structure, religious orientation and the like. I have learned to respect people within their culture without endorsing everything I see or experience there.

For example I value many African cultural features. But female mutilation is not one of them. The same is true of the traditional practice among many Indian cultures of the Suttee (widow burning). By Christian standards these cultural practices are inhumane and immoral. There may have been rational and socioeconomic reasons for these practices at one time but they do not supersede the humane reasons for banning them. I will maintain throughout that there is much to be respected in all cultures. That does not mean that everything practiced in a culture is ok. Extreme individualism in Western culture can be as dehumanizing as are honor killings in Middle Eastern cultures. Behind all cultural practices is a prophetic voice from a Christian perspective that measures all cultural forms and practices in a more Godly and human way.

INTRODUCTION

A Survivor, A Fiddler on the Roof!

There he sits, perched precariously on a rooftop, violin in hand, playing a haunting tune introducing the theme of the Fiddler on the Roof. It's one of my favorite scenes describing a life full of risk and adventure as he watches life.

Would you agree that this illustrates reality for most of us? Is not life full of calculated risks? Boarding an airplane for an extended flight; driving 75 mph on a crowded freeway; embarking on an academic program; marriage? Birthing children? Starting out on a new job?

The TV program "Survivor" is a metaphor describing what I mean. It was wildly popular for a time and exemplified a lust for danger and adventure. People were portrayed as survivors in supposed primitive and dangerous environments. Young strong bodies and minds were pitted against the forces of nature. Members of the team had as one of their goals to discredit other members, the idea being to vote people out of the community one by one. Intrigue and entrapment were common to eliminate members until only one remained, the sole survivor.

I like to think of Christian Millennials in this way, but as "Survivors in Reverse." Whereas Survivor sought to expel the weak person in the group and eliminate him or her, Christian Millennials look for ways to include the weak link and seek to help that person become stronger, thereby contributing to a community of committed strong collaborating individuals, a value wonderfully consistent with one of the core values of Millennials in general.

This is one of the things that attract me to this large and growing segment of American society.

CHAPTER 1

Who am I?

Some Millennials have referred to me as a "senior Millennial" and we laugh about it together. It's ironic when you think about it, me as an older person born the year Adolf Hitler invaded Poland (1939), thought of in some odd way as an inward, not outward, Millennial.

I'm actually a product of the so-called "silent generation," those who fought during World War II. My generation followed that Silent Generation and is referred to by some as the "Builder Generation," because it was my generation that rebuilt large swaths of Post War Europe, Asia and the economy of the United States. I've not lived a life in a typically "traditionalist" manner. Others of my generation, like my brothers, sought more traditional professional careers in engineering and architecture. While all of us were raised in a conservative Christian environment, I tended toward wanting to know more about international human behavior and what God had to do with it.

This awareness came to me in my high school biology class. The teacher had given instructions how to dissect a frog. I knew I'd be expected to dissect, pin and name its bones the next day. I prepared for the quiz. The next day arrived and she plopped the frog on my lab desk, dead of course, soaked in formaldehyde. I sliced it open and the solution flowed freely across my cardboard. I attempted to write the names of bones anyway but the ink flowed into blurry lines. When the teacher looked at it she wrote a red C on the top of the cardboard. Sitting on my stool, the thought flashed across my mind; "this frog is dead; and it died so I could get a C grade." Actually, I believe the C made a lasting impact on my life, turning me to an interest in human behavior more than impersonal science. Or so it seems to me in retrospect.

1.1 Introduction to Cross-culturalism.

A two-year stint in the US Navy followed graduation from high school. Active duty aboard an aircraft carrier took me to various cultures in Asia where I experienced first hand new and interesting worldviews and began my journey into cross-culturalism. Docking in Yokosuka, Japan for an extended refit of the ship, I traveled with a buddy to the small town of Karuizawa, in the mountains to attend a conference for missionaries.

There I was housed with a Japanese pastor who spoke limited English. I spoke no Japanese. Yet I seemed to understand the essence of what he said to his parishioners. During those few days in his small house I felt like a fiddler on the roof. The *ofuro*, (wooden fire-stoked Japanese tub bath), food and customs were all new and exciting but kept me on the edge of conflicting worldviews. Meeting Japanese people and listening to them speak a language that was new and exotic. I felt I was looking into an exotic world I didn't understand. I desperately wanted to know more.

The week ended and as we rode the train from Karuizawa to Yokosuka I reflected on these new experiences. I felt I was living on the edge of something exciting, fresh and doable. I recall looking out the train window and saying to myself, out loud, "I can do this." It was a deep inner feeling that living cross culturally was something I could do.

We returned to our ship, the USS Midway, docked at Yokosuka, and in a few days pulled out to sea for another extended tour of duty that took us from Japan to Hong Kong, south to the Philippines, and Islands in between. Each port of call introduced me to a new cultural experience; exposure to another unique Christian worldview.

At age 19 these bits of cultural experience along with God's active presence in so many different contexts brought me to a commitment. It came in the form of a book and a letter. They came to me from my parents and awaited me when I returned from my travels to Karuizawa. The letter was from my mother. She said she didn't know what God was doing in my life but perhaps this book would be helpful. The book was Betty Elliot's *Shadow of the Almighty, The Life and Testament of Jim Eliott.*

I read the book eagerly, even passionately. It seemed to me that each page was an excursion into the world I was experiencing in my travels. I was challenged to think more concretely, more about how my Christianity would actually be lived out in a cultural context different from my own.

I don't recall the exact quote but Jim Eliott was quoted by Betty saying something to the effect, "Our young people don't need a call to the mission field; they need a kick in the seat of the pants." His words jolted me. The next quote grabbed both my heart and my mind, "He is no fool, who gives what he cannot keep to gain what he cannot lose." It was this statement that put me on my knees in that small space aboard ship. The prayer I prayed I remember well;

"Dear God, I'm setting my rudder to be a missionary, but if you change the direction of this ship, so be it."

1.2 Calling

That prayer took me on a further journey of exploration. How was I to prepare for this sense of direction, some would call it "calling" in my life? Would it require schooling? And if so, where? And what subjects should I take? Bible? Theology? Missions? Anthropology? Should I go to a state university? Theological school? Bible College? My father had already told me he would help me if I returned to Dallas and attended one of the state schools there. Should I do that? And which mission structure or organization should I pursue? I met many different missionaries and observed their mission strategies. Which strategy of missions should I pursue?

I observed that different mission organizations emphasized different strategies and approaches. Some if not most tended to emphasize their parent denominations and reflected their home cultures. Others emphasized relating to the local culture. And there were variations in between. My naïve, uninformed assessment of this was it seemed best to talk about God within the context of the local culture, though I thought it might be harder to do that way. I was to learn later in my life how right I was.

I took these thoughts to my pastor when we returned to the United States. I attended Oakland Neighborhood Church in Oakland California, not far from my stateside base at Alameda Naval Air Station. I had recently learned it was a church that supported a missionary I had visited in Hong Kong. I liked what I had seen in the Chinese church there.

Chinese leaders conducted the service and though the format of the service was somewhat western it was in all other respects very much Chinese in language and other forms, much like Hong Kong culture was. The church also operated a "roof-top school" and a senior citizen center. It seemed to me that the missionary valued local culture and practiced what was then called, "social action." That appealed to me and it seemed right.

Pastor Belig listened to my story and my questions. He told me that Simpson College was just across the Bay in San Francisco, that it was a Bible College of the same denomination of the church in Hong Kong and that I should talk to Miss Riter, the registrar. Discharge from active duty was only a few weeks away so I did as he advised.

I think it's important to be open and not closed to new ideas and opportunities however novel they might appear at first. Listen to the counsel, advice of others with an open mind. Be adventurous. Say to yourself, "I think I could do this!" even if you are not sure you can or should. Inform yourself. Ask questions. Test it by putting yourself in an existential situation where you have to experience the idea. A short-term mission trip can be helpful but a longer time spent in an actual cross-cultural environment in which the focus is not so much on what you are getting from the experience but what you are actually contributing and how well you are adapting to a new and different worldview.

1.3 Training

That conversation with Miss Riter ended with me filling out an application for the fall semester, only a month away. It seemed to me that training to be a missionary in the school of the denomination of the same mission that impressed me was the right thing to do.

My father was not impressed but accepted it, as he quietly did most things.

The next four years flew by. They were full of classes, research papers, meetings, new and formative relationships, self-evaluation and experiencing new roles of leadership. That initial awareness of "I can do this" became "I wonder how best it can be done?" Leadership development was not a subject I studied. But positions of leadership provided opportunities to develop leadership skills.

I was chosen to be president of the freshman class by my peers only to be told a day later that I'd have to relinquish that role. My academic standing from High School transcripts was not high enough. Embarrassed I faced the shame of being forced to resign. Within two semesters however, I brought my GPA up and was then qualified to engage in other leadership roles to which I aspired. Later I served as the prayer band lead for Southeast Asia; then of the Student Mission Association, which included director of Pioneer Trails, a drama program. As President I presided over weekly Friday evening meetings and planned the annual theatrical production, "Pioneer Mission Trails."

My most enjoyable challenge at Simpson, later Simpson University, was being part of the Renanah Choir with Mr. Russell Marshal as director. Annual tours up and down the west coast to churches and schools taught me how to blend my voice and become one with others. The Renanah Choir was more than a college choir; it was a deep worship experience with a dedicated leader and role model.

I met Sandi at Simpson, we married and together completed all the prerequisites for the mission organization in which we were to serve. That journey took us to Thailand, Cambodia, the Philippines and to Japan from 1966 - 1999. Often, through the years we felt like that Fiddler on the Roof, playing haunting tunes, feeling as if at any moment we would fall over the edge. Nine of those years (1966 to 75) were war years on the Thai/Lao/Cambodian borders. In retrospect those years on the edge prepared us for who we are and what we are doing now.

CHAPTER 2

Intergenerational Understandings

Several years ago I met a young man at a missions network meeting. There was an immediate connection between us. We shared thoughts and ideas. I sensed in Zack a sincere and open respect for my advanced years of experience in cross-cultural ministry. Most young people, so it seemed to me, considered over 70 to be over the hill. People of my own generation often exude a similar attitude.

Zach asked questions and seemed to be willing to wait on my meanderings until I eventually arrived at the core of his interest. I was impressed. One day he asked if I'd be his mentor. I was surprised. Here was a twenty-something bright young man, articulate and intelligent asking me to be his mentor. What did I have to offer this young man with great parents and many mentors? Nevertheless we agreed to meet.

Now, it should be known here that mentoring was not a new idea to me. In my role as a visiting facilitator with Development Associates International (DAI) one of the courses I facilitated is *Mentoring and Coaching for Leadership*. There had been others God has brought my way in counseling and mentoring" relationships but none quite as direct as Zack's request.

It seemed to me I needed to be mentored and Zach was a Millennial so I could learn. He was not a secularized Millennial whom I had read and heard so many negative comments about, but a Millennial who had a graduate degree in Political Science and who was a self-confessed follower of Jesus. I suspect we have different political views but he seemed to be either disinterested what they were - whatever they might be. We committed ourselves to an open-ended mentoring relationship. In truth, my motives were a bit selfish; I wanted to know what made him tick. And I wanted to learn about the Christian Millennial worldview.

There's more to say about that relationship but in summary we both learned that the stereotypes about each other's generation though partly true were inaccurate in many ways. There was more to Zack's Millennialism (was that a new virus?) than those articles and quips than was said from pulpits and lecterns. And I like to think that Zach learned more about the "Builders/Traditionalists" than he knew before our sessions together.

2.1 These Millennials

I know. I know. There are negative stereotypes about them. They feel a need for affirmation; that they are irresponsible, they are the "Me" generation and they are captivated by technology. And there are others.

There's the positive side too. I've learned that Millennials pursue relationships intentionally, that they are positive and hopeful and that they gather information in quick and succinct ways. They are collaborative and enjoy teamwork. They have an intense loyalty to their friends. They care about the future.

It's not that I don't see the negative side of the millennial generation. I do. But I have seen the negative side of other generations too; my own builder generation for example. Its true, my generation followed the "Great Generation" and we were responsible for rebuilding parts of Europe and Asia following WW II. But there is a downside. We can be demanding, silent, hyper-individualistic and sometimes overprotective and forceful. The same can be said of other generations. All have their positives and negatives.

An old comic strip character, Pogo, comes to mind. Pogo was a forest character, an owl, known for his profound comments about life. He said once, "We have found the enemy, and they is us." Too often "the enemy" perceived is really only a perception without adequate information.

I am not part of the millennial worldview because I'm not one of them. But I understand and respect those who hold it, though not always understanding what I see there.

2.2 Communications

It's not surprising that people who live and work cross-culturally draw from cultural anthropology and intercultural communications as a means to understand the worldview of the people among whom they live and work. That being true, it's not automatic.

For example Sandi and I spent a year of graduate research into Thai culture and the cultures of Southeast Asia. This included a study of Thai language, demographics of the country and regional differences and similarities. We learned about Thai personality and behavior, religion and culture habits and such. Then we went to the Toronto Institute of Linguistics where we learned phonetics, how to make sounds in different languages, and the unique characteristics of the Thai language. We learned that language is the cradle of a culture and to understand worldview one must learn the language well.

This same principal applies to understanding all cultures and subcultures. I'm learning for example that Millennials have their own language forms and terms. A "season" of life for example is a period of time during one's lifetime and not a "time of life" as in my builder vocabulary. The difference is more than language, though the idea remains somewhat similar. Why the word "season"? It communicates something unique to this generation that other terms don't.

2.3 Learning from Millennials

My friend, Zach suggested it might be good for us to carry our attempts to understand each other's generation into a wider context. Sounded sensible to me so we did. We invited people representing different generations to come together to discuss issues from their generational perspective.

Those gatherings included Traditionalists (sometimes called "Silent" or also "Builders") (1925-1945), Baby Boomers (1946-1964), Generation X (1965-1979), and Generation Y – Millennials (1980-1995). Each month we gathered over lunch for an hour and a half to discuss relevant issues from our generational perspectives. We discussed topics such as; *Social Justice*, *Millennials & Church*, and reviewed Relevant chapters of Zack Yentzer's book, *Creative*. Others include *Multi-Generational Community, Worship, The Church and the Generations* and more. The idea that evolved was to discuss issues from within our generational perspective, the goal was to achieve mutual understanding; not to persuade others to a particular point of view.

I've found the gatherings tremendously helpful. We've learned, first of all, that Millennials are very serious and positive about the future and that is encouraging. My tendency these days is to be negative about the future and somewhat disappointed about where my culture is going. I find the desire for authentic community refreshingly Christian.

Secondly, an assumption I had of Millennials was that they would be distant and impersonal because of my age. I also assumed they would be suspicious. Instead I've found Christian Millennials to be openly welcoming and friendly.

I've also learned that Millennials we know seem to have a different sense of history; one focused on a more contemporary world than the history I knew and which shaped my life. Being a child of the 1940s and 50s, my history is one of warfare; WWII, Korea, Cambodia, Thailand, Vietnam. I've realized that my life has been shaped by world war while theirs has not.

Fourth but not last I've learned that the Millennial worldview seems to be more open to structural political/economic change than my generation or that of Gen Xers and Boomers. For example the number of Millennials who tended to move toward Democratic Socialism in the 2016 election startled me. The question still haunts me. More will be said about this later but, speaking from an anthropological perspective, it seems to me the differences are less about political and economic issues and more about the clash of Worldviews.

2.4 Worldview

Essentially, Worldview is a way in which people perceive their world, how they comprehend reality. The English term is a literal translation of the German word *Weltanschauung*. It is based largely in unreasoned, unquestioned assumptions. This does not mean these assumptions are illogical or irrational; it simply means reason or rational description is not essential to holding beliefs about life or the metaphysical.

Everyone has a worldview. It is composed of presuppositions, biases, all which are absorbed unconsciously through their cultural heritage, family upbringing, societal associations, educational environment, books, movies and media. It serves as a grid or lens though which information is filtered. Think of a fish swimming in an aquarium. It doesn't think much about the water until its removed and laid on the counter. Out of its watery environment it gasps and seeks the familiarity of its natural, indigenous, habitat. It doesn't think about its gills functioning, or the water, which passes though them. Humans are much the same.

Like the fish in water we imbibe language we imbibe language and cultural forms accepting them as normal. They even become guideposts to later reflection about things real or imagined. Seldom do we think strategically about our worldview. We simply hold it as inviolable, almost sacred and almost never do we question the core ideas and values that emanate from them.

For example, many Thai people assume that evil spirits exist, a cosmological idea, and that they control life, sickness and death. Similarly, Papuans in New Guinea and West Papua believe that every fatal disease is caused by a curse imposed by someone else, an enemy or member of another tribe or clan. The "Black magic" of some Caribbean cultures relies on the "evidence" of tealeaves or chicken entrails to determine causes of illness, death or other bad things happening in one's life.

Westerners tend to rely less on these kinds of worldview assumptions but nonetheless hold some beliefs as equally strong and valid. As a Christian I assume the existence of a personal, involved and loving God, though I can no more prove God's existence scientifically than the atheist can prove His non-existence.

If this seems a bit presumptive consider that we operate at a similar level most every day? I'm sure there is a technological explanation for the glow of a light bulb, likely written by an electrician, but for me, when I flip on a light switch, the light comes on. I have a rudimentary understanding of negative and positive leads that when connected a certain way, and then connected to a switch cause the light to come on. It's all really a matter of "faith" because I really don't get it. For me that the light comes on is a worldview assumption, an act of westernized faith.

An interesting thing about worldview is we don't question it. Told often enough, and reinforced in subtle ways, we tend to simply accept what we're led to believe. For example, I was led to believe in the 1950's that prayer in school was an ok thing, not because someone told me that, but because prayer was something that happened at school from time to time. That's no longer the case. Into the 1960s that "assumption" was challenged and subsequently altered to the overarching American view that not only is prayer forbidden in public schools but that religion in general, particularly Christianity, is not allowed.

I've come to realize that we do this politically also. For example, as mentioned earlier, I was surprised to learn that a large majority of Millennials voted for Bernie Sanders in the last presidential election (2016). Bernie is a self-identified socialist. I thought surely no one in this country would want a Socialist as the President; this is a capitalist nation. Such was the notion of a traditionalist unaware of the millennial worldview.

Traditionalists and Builders were horrified. Such was not the kind of government they had experienced. They were raised and educated during a period still strongly influenced by the age of reason and the Enlightenment. Things could be known for sure and objective truth characterized their worldview. Though the idea of relativism was not new it didn't extend to social and moral values.

Millennials, not sharing or perhaps unaware of that worldview seem ambivalent. Why not Socialism? Capitalism to many Millennials seems to be enforced greed; simply a way the rich get richer and manipulate the poor, right? Admittedly this is an overstated generalization. Not all Millennials would think this.

It could be argued that this is not a worldview thing at all. Rather it is political science; and these ideas arise from a more enlightened era. I suppose there is some truth to that, but I've been in higher education most of my adult life and have learned that there are many assumptions to many strongly held ideas, not all verifiable.

Another important feature of worldview is its function of integrating or connecting one subsystem (eg. education) to another subsystem (eg. social control). In Japanese culture, for example, there is a strong distinction between "inside" and "outside." The word *gaijin* connotes foreigner." It means those not born "under the sun" and not of Japanese blood and culture. They are outsiders.

Correspondingly this idea relates not only to the shoes one wears. A pair of slippers worn into the bathroom cannot be worn in the eating area and a pair of shoes worn outside cannot be worn inside the house. Items purchased in department stores are wrapped and then wrapped again. And so it goes. Inside/outside is a worldview conceptualization. And that idea relates to people, material items and social systems, social control, politics and religion.

Allah for example is the core of Islam as a religious system, though Muhammad as his prophet is mentioned as often in the Koran. Allah is distant, impersonal and is not truthful in the Christian sense. Allah can be deceptive as he was in the death of Jesus. It is believed that Allah would not allow a prophet to die and so a substitute was provided. Hence this perception of Allah as being deceptive in order to preserve the theology of faithfulness to his prophets is reflected in Muslim ethics and daily life so that "truth-telling" and deception can be practiced similarly. This is a core idea in Muslim theology and therefore core to Islamic worldview.

Worldview is the most difficult of all culture ideas to change because it so deeply embedded in the human experience and so widely held by the members of the culture. This is especially true of religious or philosophical ideas. For example one would think that Christianity in China should have disappeared because of the relentless efforts of the government to control and eventually eliminate it during the *Cultural Revolution* (1966-1976).

That was a move against all religion, even traditional Buddhism. The mainline 3-self Patriotic churches accommodated the government and adjusted to it while the evangelical churches refused to do so and formed the "house" church movement. Strong deeply committed pastors lead these churches. Some were imprisoned for their beliefs and pastoral roles. Has the ferocity of the Chinese government put a dent in the vibrancy of this movement? Not at all. They are dynamic vibrant family oriented fellowships. This vibrancy is obviously due to their strong belief in Jesus and a Biblical worldview they are willing to die for.

My point in all of this is to emphasize the significance and the relevance of worldview as a cultural model to help the reader to understand how cultures work. Moreover I want to illustrate the function of a biblical worldview among followers of Jesus. The same can be said for Muslims who hold an Islamic worldview and militant Hindus in India.

I see a similar kind of vibrancy among Millennial followers of Jesus on Sunday mornings at the largely Millennial church where I worship in Tucson. They demonstrate that same vibrant desire to know and follow Jesus while holding an orthodox, Reformed faith. Dressed differently than Boomers, GenXers, Builders and Traditionalists, their worship is nonetheless real, authentic and alive.

For example about 90% of attendees at Redemption are university students or recent graduates. They wear comfortable non-formal attire to worship services. The theological orientation is reformed. Presbyterian evangelicals would be comfortable with its theological orientation and liturgical format. But style and form are contextually relevant to the majority university age crowd. Most everyone participates in worship though I suppose there are some who might be distracted by technology. Still, most listen carefully to the pastor's contextually relevant messages. I've purposely looked for disinterested people during the worship and teaching times but find almost no one.

By contrast I attended a large evangelical church where most members were non-Millennials. Many dressed in more formal attire for services and during the worship time most were either not singing or just standing, as if waiting for the worship time to be over and the preaching/teaching time to begin. Many had vacant looks on their faces or were looking at their mobile phones, texting or whatever. I concluded that the level of participation was minimal.

Was this low level of participation a measure of spirituality; of some other cultural/religious value? I've concluded it's likely a combination of several things. Among them, from a cultural perspective, is that the drum/guitar driven form of worship in this older congregation is more relevant to a millennial age group. However, because that age demographic is not large enough I suspect the leaders hope that this form of worship will attract a younger Millennial set. Meanwhile the older generations in that fellowship (Boomers, GenXers, Traditionalists) on average appear to tolerate the worship time until the sermon. This in no way should be construed as critical but simply an analysis based on cultural observation.

My point is that Millennials prefer culturally relevant worship. The beat of the drum is important but so is integrity and authenticity in worship. To be clear, Millennials tend to prefer authenticity in worship to "performance" oriented worship style.

I want to emphasize again that worldview perceptions are the most difficult of all perceptions to change. This is why Traditionalists were horrified when football players took a knee at the playing of the National anthem. This to them was disrespect for the American flag, the symbol for them of national unity, pride and solidarity. It was also a disregard for a long history of positive humanitarian efforts of past administrations. The Peace Corp for example was a vision of President John F. Kennedy and was highly successful. Advances in automotive technology and electronic media can't go unnoticed. War upon war cannot be minimized. At the same time causes for those wars should not focus only on American interests. For example the American advance into Vietnam in the early 1960s was precipitated by the breaking of the SEATO treaty the United States had with the Southeast Asian nations.

It was interesting to me that the Traditionalist, Builder, Boomer and GenX generations demonstrated the most outrage and many boycotted NFL football games as a result. I didn't observe that same level of outrage among Millennials and I wondered why. Were they not as patriotic? Of is it that they lack an appreciation of American history?'

I suspect there's an element of that here but I would add that Millennials don't share a deep understanding of the worldview of those former generations. World War II, and then Korea and after that Vietnam created a deep sense of national pride and pathos among those who experienced those conflicts in some way; either directly in military service or indirectly sending their husbands and children to war; many to die there.

Millennials on the other hand arrived after those wars and do not have an existential experience with them. They learned about them either by some older friend or relative or perhaps in a history class of some kind.

To add more understanding and hopefully not confusion to the mix the political views of that period changed in higher education and among the politicians in Washington. Liberal social issues trumped (not a pun) conservative values during the Obama administration, though higher education was already trending that way. Traditional views of history, indeed the significance of history altogether, changed dramatically in most academic institutions.

Much more can be and needs to be said I suppose but what is clear from this brief overview is the development of opposing or conflicting worldviews. What is deeply significant to Traditionalists, Builders, GenXers is not so much so for Millennials. This is not because they don't appreciate that worldview; its because they don't know it. In the same way, the former generations don't really know the millennial worldview.

CHAPTER 3

Risky Advice

Something I like about Millennials is their interest in mentoring and openness to receive advice. One of the strongest emphases in the church we attend now is Mentoring. Each year a Mentoring Sunday is planned during which time those who want to be mentored are given opportunity to respond. This last Mentoring Sunday rendered 130 or so applications from a gathering of around 350 people, about 37% of the gathering. Mentors are found among the fellowship and organized so that each of the mentees is assigned a mentor. Resources are available to help mentors and effort is put into accountability for reporting.

Normally, I'm reticent to give advice. I've learned that most people really are not looking for advice. This is especially true I think among older independent minded Americans. But Millennials? That's a different story.

I mentioned Zach earlier. He asked me once if I would please mentor him through some decisions he would be making as a young single graduate from university. That request turned into a mutual mentoring process where, as I mentioned, I was introduced to the

Millennial Worldview. It became an opportunity to delve personally and in more depth into what makes them tick.

I was surprised to find young people interested in opinions about things. My older colleagues and friends grow accustomed to feelings of being ignored, of being irrelevant. I've told them I've tried retirement several times and it just doesn't work for me, it doesn't fit my "calling frame" or my still strong desire for adventure. This brings me to my first attempt at giving advice as a "Senior Millennial."

3.1 Live on the Edge!

Our second son, Scotty, lives on the edge. He and his family live in West Papua, Indonesia; the end of the world some have called it. He started and administered a study-abroad program in 1996. He called it EduVenture; short for Educational Adventure. Students from Christian colleges were invited to apply to this full semester program in which 5 courses were offered: applied anthropology, intercultural communications, spiritual formation, physical education (adventures) and community development for a total of 15 credits. The motto for the program was, *If you're not living on the edge, you're taking up too much space.*

The idea behind the program was to provide a real life experience for American Christian university students to participate in a challenging cross-cultural environment where they could grow spiritually and learn to live as global committed believers wherever God led them. It was not a recruitment program for missions; it was an attempt to provide a holistic worldview for young enquiring minds, to examine themselves in the light of cross-cultural physically challenging locations. These included Papua, Indonesia; Fiji and Mexico.

Shane applied to the program. He was, by his own admission, an inner-focused young man, tall, strong and the son of missionaries. Of the students who participated in the program I think Shane was one whom I first thought would not be not a fit. He was, by his own admission, self-centered, opportunistic and carried a "victim mentality" but he was also one who when faced with his true self was willing to change. He took easily and naturally to connecting with villagers everywhere he met them. And they seemed to be able to read his friendly accepting spirit. Shane is now in Senegal, with his wife and children, serving as cross-cultural communicators of the Gospel.

Shane is a good example of someone who came looking for fun and adventure but found a new reality in Jesus and in real human need in the process. By the end of the semester he had learned that living on the edge was more than treks in the mountains, white-water rafting, surfing or mountain biking. It was also learning to make and shoot his own handcrafted bow and arrow set as taught by his Papuan dorm mate. Or for girls it was learning how to make net bags, grass skirts, or help prepare a pit for pig-feasts by selecting just the right river rocks. The list goes on of new experiences that kept students on the edge.

And what do I mean by the edge? By edge I mean living with an excited expectation of something new and risky just beyond the horizon. It's a mixture of the known and the unknown; an excursion beyond what is comfortable and familiar toward a goal greater than what one could or would experience in one's own worldview.

I turn to the Vicar of Baghdad who captured the idea succinctly, "get rid of that American idiom, "take care," and replace it with "take risks." He was advocating only what Jesus said and modeled, "take no thought for your life, what ye shall eat, or what ye shall drink;

nor yet for your body, what ye shall put on, is not the life more than meat and the body than raiment?[1]"

These words are in stark contrast to the "American Dream" which in reality is the pursuit of material prosperity, comfort and safety. Jesus calls us to a higher purpose, a more intentional commitment to what He called "the Kingdom of God." His parables illustrate the nature of that Kingdom not as material at all but one in which the rule of God is obvious through obedience of Kingdom citizens to Kingdom values. A closer look at Jesus' descriptions of the Kingdom is about living an obedient life under God's guidance, eschewing the pleasures and comforts of the place we call home.[2]

Living on the edge is risky. Of course there is the kind of risk that is no risk at all. As in the "Survivor" TV reality program where some events are perceived to be dangerous or risky but which in reality are dramatized. In that program health workers were available, and emergency equipment ready to evacuate anyone who might be injured. By contrast real risk threatens life and limb.

I'm not advocating foolish daredevil risk taking only for the purpose of a thrill. There are limits to all things. Taking a real as opposed to perceived risk for a greater purpose than thrills or just fun is what the Vicar of Baghdad was talking about. Consider five young men, standing around a small Cessna single engine airplane parked on a beach beside a flowing river in the Amazon. They are there after a long series of attempts over several months to establish communication with this Auca tribe in Ecuador. They were known to be skittish toward outsiders, even violent and attempts in the past to make contact with them had been disastrous.

---

[1] Matthew 6:25ff

[2] See George Eldon Ladd's book about *the Kingdom of God* in *Theology of the New Testament*. A must read to understand Jesus' meanings about Kingdom life.

So why were they there? What reason did they have to undertake such a risky adventure? Was it to gain a medal? Maybe it was or could have been, but I suspect it was not a medal to hang around their necks. Rather it was to unselfishly reach out to a needy tribe with the Gospel with humanitarian overtones. Yes, there was the inner desire I'm guessing to win the approval of Jesus for whom they were taking this risk and to fulfill what they believed was obedience to their Master's command to communicate the Gospel to the "Auca Gentiles."[3] And it was real; there were no back ups, no military or security guard to insure their safety. I believe there was an altruistic goal or motivation that transcended any personal gain or glory.

Another contrasting scenario is the story of Ernest Shackleton and his exploration of the South Pole. It is a story of valor, leadership and risky adventure. This "Imperial Trans-Antarctic Expedition (1914-1917) is legendary and mind numbing. The goal was to cross the Antarctic from sea to sea crossing the Polar ice cap. Their ship, *the Endurance*, encased in ice, was crushed and sank into the icy waters leaving 100 men on the ice, loss of their major provisions and what seemed to be their doom. The story does not end that way. Instead Shackleton's at times brutal leadership lead the explorers across the ice cap, and ultimately ended their trek on two small sailing boats to the almost safety of Elephant Island.

Intriguing to me is that the expedition began with a goal of personal and national fame but the interlude of disaster altered the goal from personal and "adventure for its own sake" to a more selfless humanitarian goal of saving the lives of all 100 men. It's a true tale of selfless valor in the end.[4]

---

[3] Ephesians 3:1-12
[4] Read the full story of *The Endurance, Shackleton's Incredible Voyage,* by Alfred Lansing; or get the video series *Shackleton* by Kenneth Branagh.

Then there is the exciting story of Andre Trochme, a French Huguenot pastor. During the years of Hitler's invasion of France and his "Final Solution," Trochme and his wife Magda and parishioners welcomed and cared for fleeing Jews. When ordered by German Gestapo authorities to turn them over Trochme's reply was, "we have no Jews here, only human beings." His intense Calvinism and that of his wife allowed only a Christian definition of what was human, rejecting the notion of ethnicity as an identifying marker. It's an exciting bold story of the Village of Le Chambon and how goodness happened there.[5]

Seems to me these examples indicate what should be the purpose of adventure, of risk taking. Perhaps the greatest tale of selfless risk taking is Jesus. Stories of risky adventure abound around Him, His teaching, and His life. Take His bold excusion into the Court of the Gentiles, the only place in the Jewish Temple Gentiles were permitted to go, where He turned over tables, scourged the money lenders and admonished them not to make God's house one of "thieves."[6]

One doesn't naturally think of "mission" as an integral part of Jewish religion but there was apparently a vigorous Jewish missionary program. Boldly Jesus said openly, in the presence of lots of people, "Woe to you, teachers of the law and Pharisees, you hypocrites! You travel over land and sea to win a single convert, and when you have succeeded, you make them twice as much a child of hell as you are.[7] Risky? These leaders were influential, powerful and could at any time have Jesus arrested, which of course, later they did. Healing on the Sabbath was an intentional act of rubbing their noses in Pharisaical

---

[5] For a truly exciting tale of risk taking read *Lest Innocent Blood be Shed* by Philip Hallie.

[6] Mathew 25:13 (NIV)

[7] Matthew 23:13 (NIV)

hypocrisy, which led eventually to Jesus' arrest.[8] I could go on in this vein but suffice it to say that this kind of boldness was an adventure in "poking the bear," an intentional action to goad.

So, the first piece of risky advice I have to give my Millennial friends is don't be shy, "don't take care, take risk's," not excluding personal growth and development but also for noble unselfish purposes. Jim Elliot said it best, "he is no fool who gives what he cannot keep to gain what he cannot lose." William Wilberforce would have used different words but would not have disagreed.

3.2 Be Receptor Oriented

We might describe being "receptor oriented" the golden rule of communications. It simply means that we do all we can to understand the worldview of the person or persons to whom we seek to communicate. That means that whatever we want to communicate we should use words, symbols and ideas that are more familiar to her or his Worldview but that do not change the essential core of the message we seek to convey.

Language is a good example. As missionaries to Thailand we were required to speak and write Thai language fluently. So upon arriving in Thailand in 1966, we entered an 18-month language program. Fortunately the language school we attended used effective language learning techniques. Language was considered to be the "cradle of culture." To become effective communicators we needed to be able to speak and understand the language well. This was not a radical idea but interestingly everyone did not share it.

I heard someone imply recently that language learning is costly and too time consuming. All that is needed is to find an interpreter,

---

[8] Mark 3:1-6

plant the church and then leave after a few weeks or at most a couple of years. On the surface that idea sounds efficient. If by efficient is meant time and money it is, but it's not very effective.

We achieved a kind of 6th grade elementary fluency in Thai after 18 months of full time language study. However it took another 2 years before we felt we were really effective in the language.

Speaking the language is a huge part of intercultural connections. Learning the internal worldview assumptions and biases are essential to effective communication. For example, because Thai people are mostly Theravadic Buddhists, we read about their religious worldview as well as socio-economic systems. Moreover, by our 3rd year we learned that this "Buddhism" was realy an overlay to the real religious life of the people. That which was the more deeply held belief was *animism*, the belief that malevolent spirits hover everywhere and must be placated.

Some people considered animistic belief was merely superstition. Then there were others who took that animistic belief seriously. They believed it to be a strongly held cosmological worldview assumption without debating the realty of spirits as a truth statement. Some chose to relate to people through their language and their core cultural worldview assumptions - in this case, animistic assumptions.

The point of all this is that language and culture are complex and it takes time to learn core worldview perceptions such as God, family relationships, and to become fluent enough in the language to talk comprehensively and cohesively about them. Establishing meaningful relationships is key to effective communication, especially across cultures.

So what's my advice, not just to my millennial friends but also to non-Millennials? It's essential to get into each other's cultural frame of reference in order to understand each other.

What do drums mean to each generation? That is to say how closely connected is that instrument (form) to its audience? And why? Does the form distract from the core or essential meaning of a message? Or does the form or symbol make the meaning more clear and comprehendible? After all, the purpose of any communicational form is comprehension and not simply attractiveness.

What does wearing a tie and coat mean to Millennials and to non-Millennials when worn to a church service; to a funeral, to a wedding? Are buildings essential to the Kingdom message? What does the sound of a dropped coffee carafe in a church service mean? What is the meaning of jeans with holes in the knees, or shorts worn in church service? Does the sound of an infant crying or making infant sound lend to or distract from a service?

Do Millennials and non-Millennials know and understand the cultural frame of reference, (the cultural worldview) of respective generations? Too often we make conclusions based on inaccurate assumptions we have about other worldviews. Disunity and disharmony between generations are the consequence not of theology but on misunderstandings.

So what is my advice? Consider to whom we are communicating before we utter a word. Have a good understanding of their worldview. Ask questions, listen and learn.

3.3 Validate others but don't endorse everything you see.

How can I know what forms are valid? Are not all cultures and their respective cultural forms valid? The notion that all forms are equally valid whatever they are and wherever they are found is popular today. So if polygamy is ok for some cultures its ok for all. If it's perceived that open marriage is a valid option for some then its valid for all[9]. Given the idea of cultural relativism the question of what is valid and not valid has become vague, cloudy.

Margaret Meade popularized this notion in her anthropological work in the South Pacific Islands. Her book, *Coming of Age in Samoa,* illustrated in cultural terms the already popular notion of ethical relativism spreading though out higher education. By using informants she described courting practices and casual sexual connections among young people in American Samoa.

A New Zealand anthropologist, John Derek Freeman, discovered that her island informants were simply joking with her, something Meade didn't understand. Joking or teasing about intimate sexual information could not be disclosed to outsiders. [10]

My purpose in describing Meade's cultural fieldwork and Freeman's later analysis is to illustrate how smart people can misinterpret the realities that stand behind cultural forms. Margaret Meade was one of those very smart people. Freeman too was also smart and given later insights gleaned from his own fieldwork he was able to go beyond Meade's work. Is it any wonder that the rest of us can and do make similar misunderstandings? Later insights can help us.

---

[9] *Coming of Age in Samoa.*1928.
[10] See John Derek Freeman, 1983. *Margaret Mead and Samoa: The making and unmaking of an anthropological myth.* Cambridge: Harvard University Press

Cultural relativism essentially approves whatever ethic or value one observes in a culture. If polygamy were the norm of the culture, for example, then that would simply be a cultural value to be endorsed and practiced given a cultural relativity worldview assumption. If lying is culturally acceptable to whatever degree in the culture then it is approved given the relativistic ethic.

Cultural Validity by contrast is the notion that a culture is valid though not all the cultural practices are necessarily endorsed. For example a driver's license says nothing about values, personality or one's philosophy of life. It simply verifies that one has legal permission to drive a vehicle and that they know the rules of driving.

It's a fine line but I think the idea helps one to live with values not entirely "endorsable" by one's Christian ethic. For example, though one is raised with a commitment to absolute right/wrong moral values its possible to live among people who have contrasting or even opposite views with no immediate need to change them.

The examples I've provided are primarily taken from distant cultural environments. However I think that these principles apply to intergenerational relationships. Some of my generational friends are not congenial to the Millennial generation. It seems to me that one of the reason for that is because values and lifestyle espoused by Millennials and non-Millennials are different, as noted above in the description of Millennials.

So if intergenerational communications can be encouraged to implement cultural validity, I believe better understandings can be achieved, much like we experience in the Intergenerational Communications gatherings (IGC) each month. It's a time when we intentionally seek to understand differing points of view, trying to learn from the mistakes of others, like Margaret Mead's. She was no dummy. I see this happening all the time. Politicians make the mistake of superimposing their assumptions on the political process. Educators do it. And so do pastors. And students do it. And I have done it. But I do it less now than before. I hope this piece of advice will help you too.

3.4 Be Discerning

The age in which we live is characterized by the polarization of opinions dramatically opposed to each other. Leftism borders on a radical Marxist socialist philosophy. The radical right that advocates white supremacy/racist ideology. Then there are "moderates" and independents in between.

This is not news. It's an observation that demands careful discernment how one gets her/his information. I often feel frustrated. It seems the media I once assumed was accurate and truthful is no longer trusted. It supports one extreme or the other.

So how is one to judge? No doubt our worldview assumptions filter and to some extent interpret what we see and hear. And there are regional political and social pressures that tend to sway opinions. However, how to deal with the polarization issues concerns me. Seems to me we need to know how to discern truth from error, right from wrong and how to distinguish political and social issues.

My first suggestion toward developing discernment is to reserve judgment until contrasting views/ideas have been researched. For example, in the last presidential election I observed that Bernie Sanders advocated Democratic Socialism in his election platform. He promised free college education, free universal health care and the introduction of a Denmark form of Socialism.

Two things grabbed my attention. First that promises were made without details how these benefits would be funded. I suspect most who voted for him simply understood money for benefits would come through taxation but not nearly as much as his opponents said it would be. Nevertheless post election tabulation of voting patterns indicated most Millennials were enthusiastically in favor of him.

Aaron Blake in the Washington Post summarized it this way:

> *It's hard to overemphasize how completely and utterly Sen. Bernie Sanders dominated the youth vote to this point in the 2016 presidential campaign. While Hillary Clinton dominated him among older voters, he dominated her right back among younger voters -- even winning more than 80 percent of their votes in some states against no less than the eventual Democratic nominee.*

That Sanders was so overwhelmingly popular with Millennials surprised me. Not just because of his "Grandpaness" but because of his socialism platform. Why, I wondered, would Millennials vote for an Independent who advocated a form of Democratic Socialism?

Lots of reasons have been suggested, most of them not very cordial toward Millennials. Whitney Ross Manzo, assistant professor of political science at Meredith College in Raleigh, NC., summarized those less than complimentary comments this way, though they are not his sentiments:

> *"How did a self-proclaimed socialist win the hearts of these lazy, entitled narcissists? How could our youth be so uneducated when it comes to American politics and history?*

Are Millennials really uneducated? Manzo doesn't think so but that they interpret the world differently. His class in political science "AlterNet, Election 2016" seems to substantiate that claim. It occurs to me however from Blake's article that there are reasons more attune to the millennial worldview.

Sophia McLennan. Professor of International Affairs at Pennsylvania State University, wrote this piece in *"AlterNet, Election 2016"* titled *"Why Millennials Love Bernie Sanders: This Is What Trump, Hillary And Chris Matthews Don't Understand How Politics Has Changed."*

She quotes a Harvard study:

> *In a recent study released by Harvard millennial voters, aged 18-29, overwhelmingly favored Bernie Sanders. Sanders pulled a net favorable rating of 54 percent, Clinton only had 37 percent, and Trump pulled a miserable 17 percent of the same age group.*

Further she noted

> *"that the data, collected by researchers at Harvard University, suggest that not only has Sanders's campaign made for an unexpectedly competitive Democratic primary, he has also changed the way Millennials think about politics, said polling director John Della Volpe."*

Such are the sentiments of many toward the impact of the 2016 election, though the statistics could be massaged a bit. Still the trends seem indisputable. In my experience I find most Millennials tend to be more toward the liberal end of the political spectrum. I raise the question, why?

Sean Vasquez suggests in the Huffington Post that looking back to the deteriorating economy of the 1980's fewer jobs were available. Also the previous generation of Boomers were mired in debt and large corporations filed for bankruptcy. He cites the crash of 2007/08 and the loss of more jobs and homes. Given this worsening financial picture Millennials gave second thoughts to the more traditional ways of finance. Generally speaking they are cautious about credit card debt. Millennials are open to consider any other system than failed capitalism. They are ripe for another experiment.

Sean Vasquez points out,

> *"Surveys show that Millennials have a difficult time identifying important socialist and communist leaders of the past, such as Mao-Tse-Tung, Stalin, or Lenin — or the destruction they've caused in their countries. True, socialism and communism haven't influenced this generation's life as much as it did their parents and grandparent's generations. They have, however, been negatively affected by the mishandling of the economy by the capitalist system."*

In contrast to what has not worked very well for their parents or for them they are therefore ready to experiment with other approaches, such as European democratic socialism. Without considering the details of taxation in those contexts and with free education and universal health care touted as incentives why would they not think seriously about that?

Interacting with contrasting worldviews may not always be a pleasant experience. For example, I entered a FB page "Liberal Christians." I thought that there might be more openness, tolerance and acceptance there. However, when I began to post contrasting opinions I felt like a lion in a den of Daniels. I was pounced upon, ridiculed as if I had broken all the commandments. Less Progressive opinions and ideas were not allowed. I was shocked and dismayed realizing that liberal Christians in this FB room were far more liberal than they were Christian; that their political ideology was more significant to them than open conversation.

I learned a valuable lesson from that experience. The old "liberal/ Conservative" axis is inaccurate. It's way too broad and few people I know live at either end of the extreme. The same holds true for the terms Democrat and Republican. There are Democrats who feel their party has been hijacked by the radical left while there are some Republicans who feel there's a part of that party that has been owned by "RINO's" and who some think of as Democrats in Republican clothing. And there are Republicans positioned so far to the right that they might well be advocates of the Klu Klux Klan. It seems inaccurate and divisive to label people and treat them as an enemy when so little is known about them. What people think and believe is far more nuanced.

Dr. Paul Hiebert, one of my mentors, introduced me to a very helpful model for understanding different worldviews. It has 4 quadrants (see diagram below): (1) Closed Progressives (2) Open Progressives (3) Open Conservatives (4) Closed Conservatives. Closed Progressives and Closed Conservatives can talk with no one but those who think and believe exactly like themselves. Open Progressives and Open Conservatives however are open to dialogue with each other and with anyone who is willing and open. Here I would use the word "tolerant" in its non-politically correct meaning.

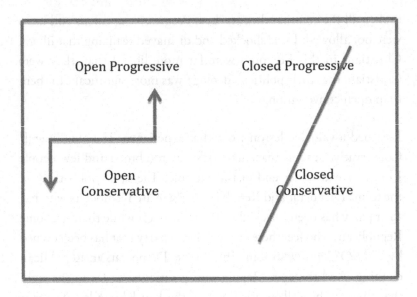

So, what is my risky advice? Do your own research and select research materials that are in contrast or in opposition to those advocated by the media you are most inclined to access. For example if mainline media (CNN, NBC, ABC, CBS, NPR, MSNBC, etc) are your first sources of information then go to those that are in contrast to them such as (Fox, BBC, Al Jazeera, etc). With regards to Internet blogs I suggest you use the same principle and that you access sites that contrast to your most avid beliefs. This may not always be a pleasant experience.

Also, open your mind without fear to new and different ideas. For Christians we have the Holy Spirit who guides. Jesus told his disciples *"When the Spirit of truth comes, he will guide you into all the truth, for he will not speak on his own authority, but whatever he hears he will speak, and he will declare to you the things that are to come."*[11] Its really true that supernatural divine direction can direct us through those difficult decisions and choices.

---

[11] John 16:13 ESV

3.5 Don't let education get in the way of learning.

Western education has a high value on credentials and academic degrees. That's not a bad thing. An earned academic degree is one indication of having mastered an area in which one wants to excel. Degrees such as these have value to indicate, hopefully, that learning has happened. In my experience the body of knowledge one masters is only a starting point. There is more to learn about that subject.

I'm into education for several reasons. First of all, I love the "light bulb moment" when comprehension happens. You can see it in the eyes. It's that moment when you see that sparkle of "I get it." It's similar I think to the feeling a child has at that first taste of chocolate. She has discovered that chocolate is much more than a picture on a poster.

One of my mentors, Charles Kraft, said "Discovery" is one of the most effective kinds of learning. He meant that learning is much more deeply imbedded when a thought or an idea is discovered more than simply heard in a lecture.

For example Thai people are a "face saving" culture. It means that being shamed in some way results in a "loss of face" or embarrassment in which dignity is lost among ones friends, family and colleagues. Guarding one's dignity is an important value in the culture and so everyone does his or her best to maintain "face." I knew this cognitively until I was invited to a wedding.

An American service man from the nearby US air base visited the church my wife and me attended in Ubon, Thailand. He met a Thai girl in the Ubon City church. Ubon is located near the borders of Laos and Cambodia. He and the girl (I will call them Bob and Noi) approached Noi's family for permission to marry. In Thailand family members traditionally arranged marriages.

So the engagement party was announced and we were invited to attend. We arrived at the time designated (6 pm) only to discover no one else had arrived, hence another lesson in learning about time in Thailand. We sat on rusty chairs and drank warm Pepsi for two hours before others began arriving. Had we not been *farang* (foreigners) we might have been "shamed" (loss of face) but being Americans I believe our Thai friends simply gave us cultural space they would not have given others.

Later that evening however, I experienced the cultural worldview in a very dramatic and personal way. One of the uncles of the bride came to our table and requested that I join him and others. I followed him into their traditional house where several men sat on mats on the floor around a kerosene lamp; the father, an uncle and some other relatives whose relationship with the family of the bride I did not know. The uncle began by subtly asking what the bridegroom (Bob) had to offer as a bride price to the family.

I knew about bride price but this was the first time I had been expected to be a *phu raprong*, or a guarantor for the bridegroom. I understood that the *phu rapron* had to pay the bride price if the groom did not. So I asked Bob how much he was prepared to pay the family. They were asking something in the neighborhood of $15,000.00. Bob's response was shock. For him this was not "loss of face" but for the bride-to-be and her family it was. To clarify, bride price in Thailand is not considered the purchase of a woman. Rather it's an indication of her value to the family. In reality it's a bonding of the future son-in-law and his family to that of the bride and her family.

In a very short time I explained this to Bob while the others waited patiently. I explained to them in Thai that this was all new to him and that he was not an officer in the Air Force and could not come up with that amount of money. However I could guarantee his heart that he would care for her and the children when they came and that he could advance around $1500.00. They talked among themselves What I learned was more than a cognitive understanding of a core worldview concept that is central to Thai culture. Briefly, it was learning experience that drove the cultural reality much deeper into my affection for the family and friends.

I've met people along the way for whom education is simply a means toward upward mobility. Now this is a fine line and I'm not dismissing the importance of gaining a body of knowledge leading to an occupation or qualifications for it. I think there is a difference between being excited about an economic theory or scientific idea and just getting by only for professional development.

Idealistic? I suppose so. I don't repent of encouraging acquiring such qualities. My advice then is to develop a thirst for knowing things, an inner love of knowledge even for its own sake. Resist the temptation to learn something only because it will get you ahead in your professional or social life. Learn to enjoy learning for learning's sake.

3.6 Expect the Unexpected.

Most people like to know in advance what is expected. We want to know, for example, what will be expected at a job or position for which we apply. A bride standing at the altar has certain expectations of her fiancé; as does the bridegroom. I bought my first car, a 1949 Chevrolet coupe in 1958. It was used, well used in fact. However I thought it was in great condition until I took my first road trip from Dallas to Louisiana. I heard expensive sounds from under the hood, When I got back to Dallas I discovered all 3 motor mounts were broken. My expectations were unrealistic.

I'm afraid that happens lots. For example, we have expectations about how we are to be treated by others. Mostly we expect to be treated fairly. We want to be respected. Being mocked or taken lightly raises one's hackles (to use a builder's generational term). We are constantly reminded that we deserve entitlements such as health care, free education, citizenship, respect, freedom from criticism or safe zones in uncomfortable political conversations, racial and gender equality, and the list goes on.

But should we? Are these expectations realistic? I suppose looked at through a sociopolitical lens one would say yes. Under the rubric human rights have been expanded from the right to life, liberty and happiness to the list above. Expectations in our contemporary life are so fine tuned, thinly cut, as to render happiness unattainable.

To make the point to my children about this I've told them, "Life for me was hard!" I walked five miles through the snow! Uphill, Both ways! Blinded by sand storms on my way home!" We laugh at the incongruity of it but I really do have a serious point. One of my sons summarizes my philosophy cryptically in the words, "Life is hard, and then you die."

I'm tempted to give a litany of hardships I've endured. I'll spare you. Instead I'll probe the idea that we deserve so very much, which to my mind, is unachievable. And even if it were achievable, I maintain that to achieve all that is not only an unreasonable expectation it is terribly unhealthy.

I don't remember the source but the maxim "we are built for adversity and not prosperity" rings true to me. I've observed that my most effective growing years were during times of adversity. Anne Bradstreet puts it this way:

"If we had no winter, the spring would not be so pleasant,
If we did not sometimes taste of adversity,
Prosperity would not be so welcome."

Poetic verse aside we see in the teachings of Jesus the expectations he had for His followers. In *the Sermon on the Mount* Jesus summarizes life in The Kingdom as difficult, the end of which is persecution.[12]

There are other passages that allude to prayer for health. There is the promise that what we ask for God will provide[13]. I would raise the question, "does getting whatever I ask for bring glory to God? Prosperity teaching is inconsistent with the reality of the history of Christianity and of life in general. Yet as a consumer society there is a tendency to evaluate most things in terms of commodities. I have a relative who put it this way; "the person who dies with the most toys wins." Seen through a consumer lens about the meaning of life this makes sense. There are many who share it.

However, when viewed through the lens of Jesus' teaching about adversity it looks very different. For example, the apostle Paul took a non-consumer assessment toward life and adversity.[14] Paul assumes trouble will be his lot in life. Instead of evaluating that on the basis of scarcity he embraces it.

He turns the argument on its head! He says that persecution; pain and poor health are qualifiers to speak into the same! To be

---

[12] Matthew 5:10,11 "Blessed are those who are persecuted because of righteousness, for theirs is the kingdom of heaven. Blessed are you when people insult you, persecute you and falsely say all kinds of evil against you because of me. Rejoice and be glad, because great is your reward in heaven, for in the same way they persecuted the prophets who were before you."

[13] John 14:13,14 ESV "Whatever you ask in my name, this I will do, that the Father may be glorified in the Son."

[14] 2 Corinthians 1:1 ff

persecuted, for example, qualifies one to speak to martyrs. It's not evangelism by the way. He also says that experiencing trouble is that which qualifies one to give comfort to those who experience trouble.

Should we look for trouble? No, it's not necessary. Trouble seems to find me, sometimes with my cooperation. No, we don't seek it to prove a point. Nor should we complain when it finds us. Or give in to the victim mentality so popular today. Whining, whimpering and wailing ones financial or health condition only makes the pain worse. I find whiners seldom meet with much compassion while those who face trouble stoically or with a sense of purpose, seem to do far better.

A final thought on expecting the unexpected. The more comfortable we are at expecting the unexpected the more likely we are to take risks. Conversely if we fear the unexpected we will be less likely to take risks. I think there is value in approaching the unexpected as opportunity. Lots of learning happens when we are surprised.

Early one morning we awoke in our house on the Campus of the seminary in the southern Phlippines to see some of our students encircling our home. We wondered what they were doing and why were they there? Shortly afterwards an officer of the Philippine Constabulary arrived. My wife and I were confused. Why were they here?

We had not been told that anyone was coming, much less an officer of the Philippine army. He told us that members of the Abu Sayyaf separatist group were seen loitering near our house late the evening before. Shocked, we knew of the Abu Sayyaf but had not expected we were in any danger. The officer explained that Tom was the target for a kidnapping and that we should leave the area.

This was unexpected news. What was even more unexpected was this group of our students who stood around our house through the night prepared to defend us in the event of a kidnap attempt! It's one thing to experience an unexpected attempted kidnapping. Ironically it's quite another to experience aid from an unexpected source.

I think it was because I had no hint of either the attempt or the source of the assistance the result was doubly impactful to us. First it drove home the reality of the danger of living in the Southern Philippines where Abu Sayyaf was active. I think the event sobered us. It was no longer just hearsay.

Second, a deeper connection evolved between my wife and me and our students. I think before this we thought of our students more academically. After this event we were connected in a more personal way. They had demonstrated a level of relationship deeper than the classroom. And for our part we thought of them as people who had placed themselves in danger, who stood between a renowned terrorist group and us. They risked their lives for ours. That made a huge difference in how we looked at each other. Our vulnerability created a softness, which they felt toward us. And their actions created in them strength, which we had not seen before.

My point is that something new can grow from both negative and positive events that we do not expect. Therefore rather than having a feeling of fear or dread I suggest cultivating a health anticipation for new and unexpected experiences.

3.7 Take the bitter with the sweet.

Professor Russ Marshal stopped our chorale practice in mid lyric and said, "people, sing me meanings!!" We all knew what he meant. It was another of his famous quips about our choral presentations. He wanted not only precise notes sung technically well; he also wanted to hear how we felt. Russ was an amazing person and choral director and everyone loved him. He was not just musically gifted; his love for God and his affection for us were palpable. So we went over that section again, this time with deeper feelings in our combined voices.

Another of his maxims was, "People, you have to take the bitter with the sweet." What he meant was that life is mixed with both positive and negative experiences and we should expect both. This was another of his brief devotionals he often gave describing his own life. We knew that he was not preaching at us. He was talking about his own life as well.

Forrest Gump (Tom Hanks) said, "My mom always said life was like a box of chocolates. You never know what you're gonna get." I liked the movie because the reference to the box of chocolates is very much like that which Russ Marshall often said.

Most people look for that box of chocolates but too often expect only the flavor we like most. Fact is there is both bitter and sweet in a box of chocolates and there is both bitter and sweet in life. Julie Andrews put it this way; "a spoonful of sugar makes the medicine go down."

I meet up with this blend of sweet and sour quite often in people I meet. Matt for example is a young man who recently experienced the death of his grand father. Now Matt's grandfather was more than just a relative. For rather complicated reasons he was like a father to Matt. He taught Matt about mechanics and life. Over a period of several years Matt watched his father/grandfather slowly deteriorate with a debilitating disease. Once strong and capable his grandfather became weak and feeble and then died. Matt was more than grief-stricken. The pain was and is now deep inside him.

Matt is a follower of Jesus. He also has lots of questions; which is a very good thing. His curious mind is dealing with loss and bereavement. Those words of the Apostle Paul, "Absent from the body and present with the Lord," don't really soothe his aching heart, his sense of loss and grief. It's a blend of sweet and sour; the sweetness of memories of a loving and caring relationship added to the reality of loss and grief. Why didn't Jesus heal him? The Bible said *"truly I say to you, whatever you ask of the Father in my name, he will give it to you.*[15]

Matt's grief placed the loss of his grandfather ahead of this passage. The pain of the present was greater than the sweet memories of the past. I think we shouldn't think less of Matt for his questions or for his grief stricken theology. Are these not the same grief stricken thoughts of Lazarus's sisters? *"Lord if you had been here...."*[16] Truth be told I suspect if we have not had these thoughts yet we will, at some point in the future.

We talked about expectations above. Another maxim applies here. Sandi, my wife, has often reminded me, "Tom, the closer your expectations are to reality the happier you will be." Somehow these connect; grief/loss and the box of chocolate; the sweet and sour. Seems to me the sooner we have a balanced view of accepting grief /loss with some form of sweetness the sooner we will come to grips with reality in a positive and productive way.

The Apostle Paul knew this. He alluded to it to his followers in that overtly pagan city of Corinth and the difficulties they faced there. He began a third letter to this growing group of Jesus followers with this admonition:

---

[15] John 16:23
[16] John 11:21

Praise be to the God and Father of our Lord Jesus Christ, the Father of compassion and the God of all comfort, ⁴ who comforts us in all our troubles, so that we can comfort those in any trouble with the comfort we ourselves receive from God. ⁵ For just as we share abundantly in the sufferings of Christ, so also our comfort abounds through Christ. ⁶ If we are distressed, it is for your comfort and salvation; if we are comforted, it is for your comfort, which produces in you patient endurance of the same sufferings we suffer. ⁷ And our hope for you is firm, because we know that just as you share in our sufferings, so also you share in our comfort.[17]

I thought it was unusual to praise God for compassion in the middle of trouble. And it would have been had the rest of the text not followed. But there is more. The "so that" which follows indicates purpose, meaning whatever trouble one experiences is for the purpose of acting compassionately toward others.

I like to think of it as acquiring an advanced degree in compassion, a credential that endorses one's ability to be compassionate. Similar to the notion of the "wounded healer," one whose wounds provide both motivation and understanding to relate to others who are experiencing that same sort of pain.

Perhaps this will help. I found myself in the Delgado clinic in Manila, Philippines with excruciating pain in my side in 1984. I thought I had pulled a muscle playing Frisbee with my boys. It was more than that. A large mass had grown and stopped the function of my kidneys. It was surgically removed and other kidney related medical issues were treated as well. Several weeks after I had recovered a friend and colleague was admitted to Delgado clinic, ironically with kidney issues. I shall always remember the feelings that rushed over me as I entered that hospital room to visit Dr. de Jesus. It was as if I had entered a sacred chamber. It was the same

---

[17] 2 Corinthians 1:3-1-7

room in which I had been, the same bed in which I had lain. I took Ben's hand and prayed.

Afterwards, Ben told me that others had visited and prayed for him but no one had prayed that day as I had. Was my prayer more powerful, more full of entreaty? No, not at all. I think it was because I had been in that same bed, in that same room for three agonizing weeks. In a sense my sojourn in trouble served as an internship in pain that created an empathetic privilege of comforting another with the same kind of comfort I had received. My advice then is to look for the purpose and not the discomfort in trouble. Its bound to come.

3.8 Build a shelf in your mind on which you place things you don't understand.

Generally I think we are inclined to dislike ambiguity. Lack of clarity and specificity can create an atmosphere of uncertainty. And so there is a sense in which uncertainty unsettles us; keeps us wondering if we have missed something? I have found this to be true about myself as well as others.

I sat on a bus about a year after arriving in Thailand waiting for others to board while scores of people passed by my window making their way to their buses. The thought crossed my mind as I sat there that nine out of ten people passing by my window were without Christ. It was a jolting realization. What I had studied theologically and resolved cognitively in my Christian college and had committed to organizationally became an existential reality in that moment on the bus.

I was then confronted with its implications: "are all these people going to Hell?" Children too? Can a person be a Christian and a

Buddhist also? Is the exclusivity of Christianity necessary? Is it true? If so how can this loving God send the really nice people I'm meeting to Hell? This existential reality made necessary a subsequent search for a theological and contextual answer. I knew if I didn't find it I'd have to confess my unbelief to my mission chairman and I knew the consequences.

So I began my theological search but this with the Thai Buddhist/ Animistic worldview as the context in my search. In time I resolved the issue. But the process is what I want to address here. I built as it were a shelf in my brain, on which I placed this question as if it were a "box" labeled "What Will God Do With This?" Over the next several months in my study and reading I would as it were reach up and take that down, open it and revisit that question. I called it my "Shelf of Ambiguity." That wasn't' the only unresolved issue in that box. There were others.

On it I placed things I needed to examine but had no ready answer at the moment. So after reflecting, praying and reading if no answer came I'd put the lid back on the box and place it back on the shelf. One by one many of those issues have been resolved in one way or another. Others remain. Some new ones have been added. Like for example why has evangelism become a negative word to Millennials? What does the word mean to them?

Lacking a carpenter to actually find a piece of Pine and literally build a shelf in your brain I suggest a less painful approach, not that it will be easier. First we have to accept the idea that not every conflict or conundrum must be resolved now. A mentor once said to me, "put your ideas on ice Tom, they'll keep." It was one of the best pieces of advice I got and it came back to me in my search to resolve dilemmas that kept creeping up in my over zealous mind.

This construction works best when you take time to sit quietly with your eyes closed and visualize yourself placing that shelf inside your head. Select the color you want it to be. Place it where you want it. But put it there and then self consciously lift your hand saying, "with this (issue) I place thee here, to rest until more light shines into the window of my soul," or some other mantra more akin to the person you are. I'm being a bit facetious here but I hope you get my drift (my meaning if my Builder's metaphor is too ancient for you).

The idea here, the purpose for this shelf is to place ideas, doctrines, political ideas, etc in a safe place. Here is why: sometimes enough is not known about a topic or an idea. So its best to put it away for a time until more information comes along. This prevents from coming to a conclusion prematurely. It provides time to do more research on a topic or idea.

3.9 Learn to live with paradox.

Paradox is defined as "… a statement that, despite apparently valid reasoning from true premises, leads to an apparently-self-contradictory or logically unacceptable conclusion."[18] Contradiction on the other hand is a combination of statements, ideas that are opposed to one another.

Too often these terms are confused and we don't observe the word "apparently" in the definition of paradox above and therefore come to the conclusion that paradox means untrue or contradictory. Perhaps we are unable to distinguish between paradox and contradiction because we haven't taken enough time to think more carefully, more deeply about the issue? Maybe we haven't built that shelf yet?

---

[18] Wikipedia.org.

I think we live with paradox unwittingly most every day. Do we really, logically, understand what happens when we flip on a light switch? The phenomena can be explained in operational terms by negative and positive leads that travel along two insulated wires resulting in illumination. However, if we think about it, it seems contradictory, logically it should not happen.

Every time I board an airplane I marvel that it gets off the ground. 100 or more people find assigned seats and store their hand luggage; most unaware of the "illogical" event on which they are engaging. Long distance international travel aboard a Boeing 747 is remarkable. Think of a Boeing 747-400. It has 171 miles (274 km) of wiring and 5 miles (8 km) of tubing. It consists of 147,000 pounds (66,150 kg) of high-strength aluminum. And yet it cruises at 550 mph. knowing this amazes me! People watch movies, read books and eat meals at 30,000+ feet above terra firma. They should be terrified! Some are but most people are unaware of the technology that keeps it airborne. The paradox is that these phenomena should not exist; yet they do.

The ideas of Evolution and Creation sat on my ambiguity shelf for several years. Then the words of Isaiah brought a degree of satisfaction, though no resolution, to my question. *"For my thoughts are not your thoughts, neither are your ways my ways, declares the LORD."*[19] I came to the point of understanding that some things are of a different category and must be understand from within that category. Can the finite comprehend the infinite? How can I, a human, warn the ants scurrying here and there that an anteater is coming? Clearly speech is out of the question. Another dimension of communication must be employed.

---

[19] Isaiah 55:8 ESV-

The sense of acceptance that this paradox held no final answer came from understanding that God is God, unique and not human. Our tendency as humans is to anthropomorphize God, to "humanize" him. That is in an attempt to satisfy human questions about ideas like God is to rid them of their uniqueness and turn them into human categories. This text relaxes that tension. The issue of creation and evolution, for me, remain on my shelf but no longer are they a heavy weight that threatens to bring the shelf down on my head.

My advice? Don't be lazy about difficult questions. Realize that for every ambiguous situation or question you resolve a new one will pop up. Celebrate that. Realize you don't have to resolve everything right away. Create a place where you can put those things that are as yet unclear and seemingly contradictory. Don't make premature judgments. Give yourself time to reflect, to explore and do your research.

3.10 God doesn't make junk and in fact He is the Great Recycler.

It was my first time to play offense. Normally I played defensive half back on my high school football team. This time due to an injury of another player I was subbed in to the right half position.

A play was called in which the quarterback handed the ball to me and I was supposed to run to the right of the right guard. To my surprise I ran through the line and gained 5 yards. I heard Coach shouting, "give it to Wisley, give it to Wisley." So play #242/pass was called. It was a fake hand off to me. I ran through the line and to the sideline and straight up the sideline to the goal line. I was to look over my shoulder and the ball would be floating down into my hands. I crossed the goal line and looked up over my shoulder and sure enough, there was the football. I extended my hands and watched as the ball fell through them to the ground. A loud whoosh of disappointment floated up from my teammates, loud cheers from the opposing team.

Though I continued as defensive halfback I never played offense again. Worse than that I often woke at night wide-awake, in a cold sweat, reliving that failed catch. It was the primary source for a long period in my life of feeling terrible about myself. I had deep self-deprecating thoughts. I failed my team. I failed myself. What would my brothers and my father think of me?

Not all my life has been characterized by one dropped football after another. I managed to hang on to a few. Nevertheless that nightmare stuck with me from age 17 into my 40s. Often I'd wake at night the image of that dropped football as stark in my mind as the day I dropped it. It became a symbol of failure, or the fear of it. I felt like junk.

I've discovered that fear of failure is a common theme among many. Our tendency is to let past failures define us. But should it? Indeed past failures provide rich soil for future successes. I suspect you've heard this before but really! It's true. For example, Thomas Edison tried more than a thousand times to make a filament bulb. A reporter asked him whether Edison wasted his time. Edison said, "No I just found a thousand ways in which I could not make the filament bulb."[20]

In my own situation while the dropped football was troublesome it was also evidence that perhaps my skill in that game was in other areas. I focused on becoming a better defensive halfback. Eventually I earned the confidence of my teammates and they voted me captain for the defensive team. Primarily because I demonstrated proficiency in making decisions under pressure about accepting or rejecting penalties.

---

[20] Sited in English for Students, "*Failure is the Stepping Stone to Success.*"

I had self-image issues. My self-image was reinforced by names given me in humor but nonetheless degrading and damaging to my sense of self-value. I earned the label "old blind Tom" because at age 9 to 12 I tended to run into a coffee table in the front room or other objects situated here and there around the house. I was called "little Wisley" by my teammates, referring both to my stature and by being the younger brother. It seems in retrospect I was always catching up, or at least trying to.

I think Coach Brown saw my struggle. He was also my math teacher. One day he called out to me in the middle of a practice. He said something to the effect, "Wisley! You're gonna be Doak from now on." I was pleased but surprised. Doak Walker was the quarterback for Southern Methodist University. He too was small but his determination, fearlessness and skill is what he was known for. I think Coach Brown saw those qualities in me and that made all the difference in how I saw myself.

God as the Creator sees us that way. I think we see that in the Creation story. Genesis ends the creation account with the words *"And God saw everything that he had made, and behold, it was very good."*[21] Those are pretty imposing words. Of course that was "pre-fall" language. Things changed dramatically after that. Adam and Eve engaged in a blame game with each other, even blame directed towards the One who created them! Ever since we have blamed each other and God for self-made disasters. Thing is if we read the Genesis account carefully its clear that God is gracious toward both and both were complicit is disobedience. They were hiding! "Adam, where are you?" is less about God not knowing where they were and more about knowing what they had done and God lovingly calling them out.[22]

---

[21] Genesis 1:31 ESV
[22] Genesis 3:9

Shame added to their sense of loss and ensuing self-loathing. Their failure must have made them feel less than what they had been. Yet God had said, "it is good," meaning all of creation. They remained created beings, still in the image of God; albeit changed. They were not junk. I think we see here God as the great recycler of damaged goods.

There was a pond not far from our home in Thailand. A lovely Lotus flower floated on top of dark still water. Thailand being a Buddhist country I discovered that the Lotus flower was a symbol in Buddhist thought of purity. And yet, below the surface of that pond? I found deep muck, old plastic water bottles, broken glass and other non-descript items, stinky and smelly. I can't help but think of that Lotus pond as a metaphor of life. Out of the muck and mire of life, loss and garbage grows something beautiful and at times fragrant, like the Lotus blossom.

What is the "junk" in your life? Is there a pile of stinking stuff hidden away in your house? Is there a need for some form of spring-cleaning in your life? When we repent of whatever it is hidden away God not only forgives and cleanses He also makes of that heap something beautiful. The person who has been sexually abused can because of that abuse become the wounded healer for others who have experienced the same.

Teo van der Weele was sexually abused as a child when he lived in an orphanage in Holland during World War II. You can read his story in his book.[23] The abuse he endured as a child could have led Teo into a life of abusing others or perhaps other forms of abusing himself. Instead Teo turned the comfort he found in Jesus into schools for training others to deal with sexual abuse.

---

[23] *From Shame to Peace*, April 7, 1995, Teo van der Weele.

I've learned that God does not make junk but that he takes what we consider to be junk makes beautiful things with it. My advice? Whatever you think is junk in your life give God the opportunity to transform it into something beautiful. He does that all the time. But I think for that to happen we have to open the door of access to it.

3.11 Avoid engaging people who are closed.

It goes without saying that we are living in an era, or we can call it a season, of political and religious polarization. People seem to be on one side or another of a political/religious divide. Not long ago I saw this Face book page, The Liberal Christian. As an open conservative I thought I might find some one to exchange ideas with since it was a Christian and the Liberal FB site identified also as Christian.

Naïveté is a wonderful thing. It's the stuff that makes one go where angels fear to trade. So I went in and raised the topic of abortion thinking naively that it would be a safe subject. My naiveté gave me a false security that even though most in the room would be liberal politically their Christian orientation would prevail and most if not all would be pro-choice. I should have hearkened to my wife's admonition; "Tom the closer your expectations are to reality the happier you will be." Immediately I was pounced up as being opposed to women's rights and accused by other mainstream feminist epitaphs reserved for non-thinking redneck uneducated oafs. I resisted for a few moments but soon left the FB room, chastised by the pro-abortion mob.

What did I learn? Several things. First and foremost I learned that its possible to be more political than Christian. Second, I left the FB page pledging that I be more Christ like in my responses to those who hold political and social views different than my own. Third I am determined to not let worldview assumptions in contrast to mine become a barrier to relationships. I've discovered that I don't have all the information about some topics or positions and that others can help fill the gaps in my knowledge bank. And finally, to refer back Dr. Hiebert's 4-quadrant model engaging open liberals and conservatives and avoiding those who are closed (see 3.4). By "avoid" I mean avoid acrimonious debates. They are meaningless.

3.12 Questions are better than statements.

I read a book several years ago that reminded me of something that lay dormant within me. I think I knew that asking questions usually resulted in better conversations but this book made me think more deeply. *Socratic Circles* was written primarily for teaching middle and high school students critical and creative thinking skills. The book altered my approach to teaching.[24]

I think I had always known the value of questions that enhanced student interest in a subject matter. But this book helped organizationally to implement a method of teaching that minimized lecture and enhanced learning using a Socratic approach. As a teacher I wanted to find a way to reduce student apathy and increase active involvement in the subject matter. So arranging groups of 5 to 8 students and posing meaningful questions encouraged them not only to pursue a line of thinking but also encouraged them to respect other perspectives.

My purpose is citing Socratic Circles is not to promote this particular pedagogical method or the book. Rather I want to encourage the use of questions in communication. Questions encourage openness and dialogue. For example, it might be better to ask, "What do you think about an unexpected pregnancy? What options do you see? And then

[24] *Socratic Circles*: *Fostering Critical and Creative Thinking in Middle and High School*. Matt Copeland, 2005.

wait for a response. Wait long enough to hear the other out. And then I've found its best to wait for an invitation to give a response.

Am I consistent in following my own advice? Too often I've not been. I'm inclined, too ready to express my own opinion too soon. I find I need to suppress this inclination and consciously focus on the other. Nevertheless I encourage it for all. Don't you agree?

3.13 Receptor oriented communication is better than me-centered.

I didn't realize how "me-centered" I could be until a mentor suggested receptor-oriented communication. What he meant was that I should consider the cultural worldview of the person with whom I'm communicating and that I should frame my communication with her or his culture foremost in my mind. He didn't mean that the message needed to change but rather that the forms more natural to the receiving culture should shape the core message to produce comprehension of the message. The key word is comprehension.

Too often I'm tempted to be "me-centered" or "my message centered." I have to confess that what I want to say often seems more important. That, I think, is because I can be egocentric. Also, the message is important. So I want to communicate that message and its implications to the person.

The importance of the message often takes precedence over the receptor of the message. An evangelistic enterprise produced the "gospel blimp," an indiscriminant dropping of thousands of gospel tracts from a dirigible over an unsuspecting community. People meant well but they didn't consider how invasive leaflets would be that floated from the sky into swimming pools, yards and public streets.

And there is this; within the first 15 minutes of a conversation: "Do you know that unless you repent and confess your sins you will go straight to Hell?" A comment like this is message and sender oriented and is likely to produce rejection of the message and the sender.

Some of the deepest needs people have are acceptance, kindness, understanding. Telling the person he/she is on the way to Hell is not affirming nor does it seem true perhaps from within his/her worldview. I'm not suggesting that the truth of heaven or hell be changed because that idea is not within the framework of truth as perceived by the receptor. I'm suggesting something different.

Hendrik Kraemer observed that different religions hold ideas that are common to other religions[25]. He didn't say they were the same. They represent potential "contacts" of one religion with another. He talked about "common goals" different religions have with other religions; such as alleviating suffering and serving the needs common to people everywhere. Common to most people is a need to be treated with respect regardless of gender, faith or ethnicity. These human needs have different cultural forma of expression and different intensities. Not only these kinds of needs there is also the need to have one's way of life respected.

Paw Kean sat across from me at a small table in a traditional noodle shop in Northeast Thailand. Others sat around tables talking quietly, sipping coffee and beer, eating noodles. Paw Kean was an older man, in his 50s. I was in my 30s. I had asked Paw Kean, a retired Thai schoolteacher, in a former conversation about the process of decision making among Thai people. His answer was a request that I take this trip with him.

We slurped our spicy noodles and in between he explained that Thai people characteristically make decisions as a family. In general he

---

[25] *The Christian Message in a Non-Christian World.* 1977. Kraemeral.

said decisions were made by the family and not by individuals. A nephew of his wanted to buy a car to be used as a taxi. So he went to his mother, the person who influenced decisions to be made in the Thai household, and asked for her permission. She then went to her husband, the father and decision maker for the family, and explained what their son wanted to do. The father in turn went to other family members, his brothers and others, and discussed the request. Eventually an agreement was made in which the money to purchase a car for the purpose of running a family taxi business was given and further agreements of shared revenue were worked out among the family members.

The decision making process might seem, tedious but for my Thai teacher friend this was the way it was done in his culture. It was part of the traditional way most decisions were made. In retrospect I believe that bowl of noodles and my sincere curiosity to understand Thai culture were the ingredients that formed this relationship of trust. An honest query and sincere desire to know his culture communicated respect. This is what is meant by 'receptor oriented communication."

That principal holds true among sub cultures as well. Immigrant populations from Asia, Middle East, Africa and Latin America to name only a few are present in the United States. Some have immigrated legally. Others are asylum seekers. Some are undocumented. They are no less of their indigenous cultures though they are to greater or lesser degrees integrating into one of the sub cultures in the United States. They are in need of respect just as we would be had we immigrated to their home culture.

It needs to be said again that to respect people is not necessarily to endorse everything about their culture. Some things shouldn't be endorsed or accepted. I respect Indian Hindu culture but I can't accept as valid the *suttee* (practice of widow burning). I love many

African culture traits and practices. But tribalism is a huge problem that separates one group from another based on ethnic identity. It's a form of racism, which by the way is endemic among virtually all cultures. The so called "noble savage" who is devoid of all cultural judgments is a myth born in the minds of cultural anthropologists who have filtered their observations through the grid of ethical relativism.

Let me remind you that honest questions about cultural practices are better than statements against them. If a relationship has been cultivated over a period of time and cultural practices are being discussed then a question about the practice might render a discussion about it. I've learned that an honest question is usually not embarrassing. A sincere comment like: *"Your head covering is beautiful; do you mind? What is the meaning of it?"* Genuine sincere questions seeking information reflect respect and will help toward genuine relationships.

Subcultures have regional cultural uniqueness's. Southerners in Georgia and Westerners in California have different cultural practices and linguistics expressions. Often people don't respect or acknowledge these as regional practices. It's easy to think of America as a melting pot that produces "Americans" as a homogenous people who are all the same.

Nothing could be further from the truth. People in Appalachia are often described by outsiders derisively as "Hillbillies." Pima Indians were once referred to as *Papago*. It means "bean eater" and so was rejected as a derogatory term replacing it as *Tohono O'odom*.

There is another level of sub culture. Millennials, for example, are not the same as Traditionalists. And Boomers are distinct from GenXers. There are language differences, such as "adulting" among Millennials being equivalent to the expression "grow up" among

GenXers. Also worldview assumptions like "why not socialism? Capitalism is greed" among many Millennials contrasted to "Socialism is Communism" by those who lived through the cold war. These are not just linguistic and historic events foci. They are representative of significant worldview differences.

We learned earlier that comprehending worldview across cultures is difficult and that the core ideas of worldview are difficult to change. Which is why concerted efforts have to be made to "get it."

For example several years ago my wife and I were asked to help bring some understanding to three generational Japanese culture groups in Los Angeles; "*isay, nisay, sansay.*" The first generation (*isay*) Japanese had immigrated to the USA but did not learn to speak English fluently. They valued traditional Japanese values and culture while acculturating to their new American culture. Second generation Japanese (*nisay*) didn't hold the same traditional Japanese values of language and didn't really try to learn it. They were enculturated into American culture and spoke English Fluently. They had little interest in traditional Japanese culture and some even seemed to be in reaction to it. Third generation Japanese (*sansay*) seemed to reflect interest and appreciation for traditional Japanese culture but appeared to be culturally American in language and culture. There seemed to be a nostalgic appreciation for the history and worldview of traditional Japanese culture.

My wife and I spent a Saturday with this three-generational group. The task appointed to us was to bring some understanding and intergenerational communication between them. We did this in several ways.

First we gathered everyone together in an icebreaker session. It was during this time we learned more about specific generational conflicts among them. Some being *isay* had little to say but their demeanor spoke volumes. We gathered that the younger generations struggled to appreciate them. We detected hurt, misunderstanding and isolation. *nisay and sansay* were more verbal and animated than the first generation. We sensed deeper understanding and compassion toward the *isay* from the *sansay* toward the *isay*.

Then we did some small group interactions around tables. The tables were arranged so that the generations were mixed together. We wanted them to start talking to each other. At the end of the day I introduced the concept of worldview and gave them our assessment. I don't know to what extent generational conflicts were remedied or lessened. However the sessions were cathartic and the conversations around the tables were animated, especially among the second and third generation Japanese. A greater degree of understanding and appreciation for each other was achieved.

I've emphasized the importance of Intergenerational communication and it might seem a distant reality to many. The popular notion is that it doesn't happen very often. I've hinted as much above with regard to the Intergenerational Communication Gathering (IGC). According to Barna:[26]

> Two-thirds of Americans (68%) say they have a close friend who is either 15 years older or younger. A quarter of Americans (25%) has an older confidant, while fewer (16%) have a younger friend. Of those who enjoy multigenerational friendships, the plurality (27%) reports having *both* older and younger friends. Women are especially likely to report intergenerational friendships, usually with older peers (31% vs. 19% of men).

---

[26] Research Releases in Culture & Media, March 12, 2019

I was pleasantly surprised at the Barna research. I wasn't prepared for my limited experience to be so different from expectations. And yet that seems to be the case. Very often perceptions based on our personal experience are not substantiated by the facts.

Receptor oriented communication is a self-conscious effort to purposefully seek to understand the worldview of another person and to take steps to shape our communication around mutual respect and understanding. It's far better than always trying to convince others of our perceptions and values. I recommend it.

3.14 Don't burn your bridges; you might have to cross them again.

If the time hasn't come yet it will someday when you will become dissatisfied or disillusioned with a job or a relationship; maybe a position that you've accepted. Perhaps you've been enfolded in a group and you've become dissatisfied with some aspect of the group; its leadership or some members of it. The inclination we have in situations like that is to stomp off in a rage, burning the bridge behind us.

It's true. There are situations when the time has come to move on. Perhaps the situation you signed on for has changed; you've lost confidence in the supervisor. Trust has been broken. Or perhaps another person got the promotion you should have gotten therefore dashing your hopes for future advancement.

I'll call her *Aimisan*. She was a young Japanese woman, 26 years of age and had accepted a short-term mission assignment from her home church in Japan to Indonesia. While there she had fallen in love with the people and culture and correspondingly the Javanese people had responded to her humility and sense of order, kindness and generosity. Her short-term assignment completed she was invited to return in a more full-time capacity. Elated she returned to Japan to report and request the church to support her in prayer and financially.

We need some background. In Japan the Pastor of the local church is often considered much like the boss of a corporation or business. So characteristically her pastor being of an older tradition refused her request. His reason? He felt she was needed more in the local church than she was in Indonesia. She repeated her request and again it was denied. It was at the point we met *Aimisan* at the international church at which I was the pastor. She was disappointed, feeling her life goals had been thwarted and disrespected. Being Japanese she understood the traditional role of her pastor but she had changed. She had become bi-cultural and committed to her mission work while her pastor remained traditionally mono-cultural committed to his small flock.

Her dilemma? Was she to leave her church? Burn her bridges so to speak and find support from some parachurch organization? We advised her to do her best to remain loyal to her local church and to try to get the church organization in Indonesia to write to her pastor requesting directly for her return. We left Japan before this was resolved so I don't know the final outcome.

Perhaps you've had a similar experience? Torn between loyalty and an exciting new vision, work or ministry? How will you make the transition? Several options present themselves. Often the first inclination is to find a reason to leave so that the new opportunity can become a reality. We might be tempted to find someone to blame. Or the conditions of the work might have become more than you can handle so you feel you must escape.

Whatever the cause for a necessary change we should try our best not to leave a job or ministry that leaves scorched earth behind; meaning angry feelings or forced resignation. The idea is to leave positive feelings about the work you have done in the wake of any work or ministry done there. This might include not rocking the boat about personal issues that have nothing to do with the policies of the institution. Or it could be a personality conflict with a superior? Or maybe it's a conflict in the philosophy of the organization that you can no longer support? How do you effect this change?

There will be standards of separation unique to the respective organization and you will have to handle those as best you can. Behind those standards however is the advice given me by my friend Don Scott: "never burn your bridges Tom; for someday you may have to cross that bridge in some form." It was good advice and I have tried to follow it as best I can, though not always successfully. Still it's been a positive goal to have before me in the changes I've had to make over the years.

I've made more changes than planned but most were forced by circumstances. For example we went to Thailand in 1966 planning to serve there as missionaries until retirement. The Vietnam War and attendant mission needs and strategies of our mission agency changed that. Those changes had a rippling effect that took us to Cambodia and then when Cambodia fell to the Khmer Rouge we returned to the United States. After completing further graduate studies we were assigned by our mission to a seminary in the Philippines. Health issues forced our return to the USA following extensive surgery and an extended furlough of five years teaching at a university in the United States. When I interviewed for that position at the university one of issues raised by a monocultural interviewer was about the frequency of changes on my vita. I felt misunderstood, even offended, that this vice president of a top university could not put together the obvious reasons for these changes. Those who could not grasp the nature of interdisciplinary and intercultural missionary work plagued my tenure at that university with similar issues. Leaving there to return to Asia to a Japanese university was a huge relief.

Stressors we have had but nothing that affected an organizational breech. What I want to encourage is that you follow my friend Don's advice to me. Don't burn your bridges behind you. As best you can leave them intact. You will meet people from those organizations or ministries again some day and that meeting should be characterized by good will.

3.15 Don't let lack of planning create an emergency for others.

We worked together as a family in an educational adventure study abroad program for American college students. The study center was located in Papua, Indonesia. Scotty, our second son, was the creator and director of the program. He had just informed his older brother Dan of yet another change in scheduling plans. This change presented another irritating adjustment in Dan's already tight schedule to his teaching assignment and to his family responsibilities. Frustrated, Dan's response to his visionary brother was, "Scotty, your lack of planning does not represent an emergency for me."

Does this sound familiar? Most everyone has been on one end of this conversation at one time or another. I have been guilty at both ends. I have caused annoyance and have experienced the same as a result of either poor planning or unavoidable changes in circumstances.

What can or should one do? For starters it occurs to me that it's good to think of interruptions as opportunities for the cultivation of patience. It's a good start. Maybe you've heard this before? "Be careful what you ask, or pray, for because you might get it?" It's true.

Every prayer for patience, for God's intervention in some plan, there might also be a silent imbedded prayer for change in plans that were not anticipated.

One of those unintended consequences happened as most do in an unexpected way. A group of VIP's from the United States was visiting the seminary at which I was the Academic Dean in Manila, Philippines. A luncheon was planned at a restaurant in Manila. I instructed the Business Manger, George, to arrange it. As we were exiting the seminary to the parking lot I asked him at which restaurant had he made reservations? Embarrassed he informed me that he had forgotten to do it. In anger I lashed out, "George!!! That was YOUR JOB!! Embarrassed George looked down and rushed away. Immediately I knew I had caused George to lose face among all these dignitaries and friends. Immediately I regretted my loss of temper and impatient reaction. I looked for George the next day but he was nowhere to be found. Without informing me he simply packed up and left town not telling me where he was going or leaving a forwarding address.

My uncontrolled reaction was the cause of George's departure. I should have checked on these plans a day or two earlier. My lack of planning represented an emergency for George and ultimately his embarrassment and loss of face. I've sought to apologize several times since but George remains elusive. I learned a lesson the hard way and at the expense of a good man.

3.16 Life isn't about how often you fall.

If you live in icy conditions it's more about how often you get up then how often you fall. After failing in temper control with George I began to wonder why I often, almost predictably, reacted as I did? This was not the first time I lost my temper. And why had this become a pattern in my life? I pointed to obvious reasons: heritage, ancestry, upbringing, social anxiety, athletics; and if I self reflected long enough could come up with more reasons to blame for my propensity to my loss of temper.

Once I was in a self-analytical mode about why people did what they did. one of my sons listened intently, then said, "Dad, its just sin." That hit a nerve. He was right. I had not acknowledged the basic nature of my propensity. I would like to say that was the end of it; that cognitively acknowledging the basic issue in my life was enough to put me on the road to control. It wasn't. Not until the *Crucible*.

The *Crucible* (*Dare to Soar*) is a weekend with men who struggle with issues in their lives. Among them for the weekend were those overcoming anger issues, some with sex or chemical addictions and others who just needed to get in touch with their inner person. It was an eclectic group of men, all committed to overcoming some issue in their life. We had that in common. Also what we had in common was more than a weekend seminar or workshop listening to another lecture.

Instead it was a weekend where we bared our souls to each other in confidence among leaders skilled in helping us face our fears and addictions. For me it was the moment I stood in front of a man and saw in him my mother. It was the moment she had her emotional collapse; her eyes were wild, her face terrified. I was maybe five to seven years of age and my brothers and father were standing round. It was that moment that flashed before my eyes and which became the focal point of the weekend for me. It was the image with which I wrestled over the next two days.

I don't want you to misunderstand. I did not consider my mother to be an evil person. Nor do I blame her for the anxieties I felt and which made me vulnerable to other stressors in my young life. But it was the source, so it seemed to me on that weekend, the well from which I had inadvertently drawn. Perhaps this poem best describes what happened and illustrates better than narrative what happened to me.

Daring to Soar O'er Ketchikan Bay

I sat alone in a comfortable chair
Observing a scene, seemingly placid - serene.
By the shore of Ketchikan Bay.

An eagle, regal and strong, sat
Perched atop a tall pine tree,
By the shore of Ketchikan Bay.

I watched as it soared,
Transfixed as it landed
On the waters of Ketchikan Bay.

It fought and it struggled to pull
This grand fish, too large, too heavy to lift,
From the waters of Ketchikan Bay.

Again and again in a futile fight
Vain was its effort to fly;
From the waters of Ketchikan Bay.

Flapping its wings, straining
It dragged its prey
Through the waters of Ketchikan Bay.

Sinking beneath waters, icy and cold
But cheered on by once strangers
I made it to shore, of my own Ketchikan Bay.

Panting, exhausted, I stood o'er my prey
My talons released from this dead, dread thing
I once thought I wanted to eat.

Buried instead, with one last look
I hopped, skipped and jumped, and spread my wings
And soar again, over the waters of my Ketchikan Bay.

That which brings me to this piece of risky advice is the importance of getting up, again and again, after slippery falls. It's kind of uncomfortable laying in the cold wet snow feeling sorry for one self. Doesn't it make more sense to pick oneself up and try again, even if the sidewalk is still icy?

3.17 Trust God, love people, use things.

The tendency in secular materialist societies is to "use people, love things and question if God is real? Does he or she really exist? The emphasis is on things, a preoccupation on material acquisition. I have a relative who summed it up like this; "he who dies with the most toys wins."

This preoccupation with stuff is common. It's a human thing that arises from the need to eat, work and play; to go places and do things. All cultures create and maintain socioeconomic structures for those purposes. In Western cultures free enterprise capitalism is one socioeconomic approach and one which the reader has had broad experience. Another is socialism in its various forms and applications such as Democratic Socialism as in some European countries like Denmark, Sweden and others. This form is sometimes referred to as "gradualism" because the transition from its former socioeconomic structure is gradual but like all forms of Socialism leads to centralized state control of good and services.

Then there is Marxist/Leninist Socialism sometimes called Scientific Socialism such as in Russia (Leninism) and China (Maoism). This form transitions ideally according to Marxist theory by violent overthrow (revolution) of the existing order and enforcement of centralized government control of goods and services.

There is also what some have called Third World Socialims, applications of Marxist theory applied to their cultures in a more culturally relevant way. These include Cuba, countries in Africa, the Middle East and some island nations. Essentially they are cultural applications of Marxist theory.

This is not a study in economics. I site these only to indicate the preoccupation human beings have on stuff. It's not my purpose to laud one arrangement as good and another as bad. There are strengths and weaknesses to each. But a preoccupation with things as apposed to non-things like people and how we treat them is important, especially to the follower of Jesus is this true.

I'm convinced that this distinction is one Jesus made and which set His teaching apart from others. He said that a person cannot serve two masters, God and mammon (money, material wealth); that we always will choose one or the other.[27] Confronted by a young man who wanted to know how to get eternal life Jesus said he should give his wealth to the poor and follow Jesus. I suspect the young man wanted to know how to maintain his comfortable life style because the text indicates he was very wealthy. Jesus' answer was not satisfying. Giving his stuff to the poor was not an option.[28]

But it was an option for many who followed Jesus and who applied His teaching. The core of Christianity is found in what has been

---

[27] Matthew 6:24
[28] Matthew 16:19-24

described as the Sermon on the Mount.[29] And many there were who found what Jesus said and modeled to be better than the pursuit for wealth and stuff. The book of Acts records how that teaching invaded the hearts and lives of a significant number of those early followers. The record is found in the book of Acts.

> *"Now the full number of those who believed were of one heart and soul, and no one said that any of the things that belonged to him was his own, but they had everything in common."*[30]

Its not known how long those early believers lived that way. Apparently they shared all things in community for a season. This was not the establishment of a political party or the formation of its socioeconomic structure. There is no historical evidence that it became some primitive form of communism as some have advocated. Rather it was a total change from selfishness to a community of people who implemented the teaching of Jesus, to love others and care for them more than one self.[31]

Love people

Some people think of Love as a rosy feeling one has toward another. People also talk about chocolate that way. In addition that popular notion of love is used in a variety of ways and has several meanings. There's the kind of love friends have one for another (*phileo*). And then there is that raw gut erotic feeling one has for another originally designed to produce intimacy between two people as a kind of basic human glue to keep them together. God was on the scene when He

---

[29] Matthew 5-7 see John Stott, Martyn Lloyd Jones, *Studies in the Sermon on the Mount.*

[30] Acts 4:32

[31] *"The Golden Rule,"* Luke 6:31

put us together as a species and demonstrated a third kind of love (*agape*) as a means to bring discipline to the other two.[32] *Agape* is a choice to love self-sacrificially. In this sense it's a contrasting love to the other two in that *phileo* and *eros* can be and often are more self focused.

To these three forms (C.S. Lewis) added a fourth, *Storge* an empathetic love as in a family. It's a kind of love that binds people together in familial ways that the other three don't. Its kind of bound up in the phrase, "blood is thicker than water." It seems family members will forgive trespasses more quickly than they will forgive or understand spouses, friends or sexual partners.

What's the connection? Its significant to me that we love people in ways that are deeper and more connected to our inner selves than any affection we might have for a new car, the purchase of a home or some new electronic gadget. Things are to be used. People are to be loved, valued and cared for in ways that are different than things. It's this difference that makes Christian community so very different from a community brought together for political or purely social purposes.

Its telling to me that people who congregate for a political agenda tend to break apart into competing factions when political issues change or are altered. A community that congregates within an environment of *agape* love is more resilient and has within it the capacity to endure breaking apart because a common bond holds that community together. This is not to say that political and social pressures will not at some point be exerted and threaten sometimes cause that community to shatter. I'm convinced that happens when an *agape* community moves away from its *agape* essence and operates as only a social or political entity.

---

[32] See C.S. Lewis, *The Four Loves.*

Much is said about respecting people, not offending them. Especially is this true about ethnic minorities though not much is said why people should be respected or disrespected beyond the color of their skin or one's political affiliation. I think being offended is really a violation of one of those four loves rather than one's ethnicity? But often respect is withheld ostensibly because of one's ethnicity. Always there are other factors cited for not respecting others.

This is a generalization but I think it holds true. At one time in American culture pastors and churches were greatly respected by the general population. In recent times both leftist and conservative Christians are mocked and thought of as uneducated and unsophisticated. As globalization and secularization grow the influence of Christian belief and practice lessens in the general population.

In Asia Korean people are generally looked down upon by Japanese and not permitted to purchase property in Japan because they are outsiders to Japanese culture. Koreans for their part remember the brutal Japanese colonization of Korea during World War II. The use of Korean women as "comfort" women (forced prostitution) to Japanese soldiers during that war has not been forgotten.

In Africa it appears to me from my limited experience that Tanzanians tend to view Nigerians as overly aggressive while Nigerians generally view Tanzanians as lazy and non-assertive, mutual disrespect for each other's cultures. Tribalism in Africa is among the strongest contributors to division and disrespect. Only among followers of Jesus is there effort toward *agape* relationships among tribal groups. The concept of mutual understanding and sharing is simply not there apart from Christian groups.

I could go on in this vein for sometime. Examples abound everywhere of the power of politicized ethnocentrism that destroy human community and render people at odds with each other. In my view this is one of most difficult of all issues in America. Ethnocentrism has always been a force to deal with in trying to bring different ethnic groups together in the United States.

Initial immigrations historically from Italy, Scotland, Ireland and England created a cultural vegetable basket. Those ethnicities added to the already existing indigenous cultures of Cherokee, Algonquin, Apache, Pima and many other tribal groups and presented huge cultural diversity to this newly established country. Add to that cultural diversity, highly charged political differences and a form of politicized ethnocentrism has evolved that threatens to turn the United States into the Ununited States. Accusations of ethnic disrespect based on historical antecedents of slavery revive latent negative forces that pit blacks against whites, blacks against Hispanics, Democrat Progressives against Republican Conservatives.

Moral disintegration has clouded issues of sexuality; maleness and femaleness, sexual identification that pits gay people against straight people. The issues would be complex enough but they have turned a corner into what is politically correct and incorrect. People are abused, mocked and culturally disenfranchised based upon their political orientation. As is said so often at our church, this is not as it should be. What's the answer?

Trust God.

I take God seriously, that He is real and that He is involved in my life and in the lives of others both near and far. I believe this because I see no evidence that He doesn't and plenty of evidence that He does. I know its vogue to doubt the existence of things one cannot see from a materialist worldview. And I know that it has become unpopular to be Christian in today's pluralistic worldview.

However it's those things that reinforce my faith. I think it's also part of living on the edge, the adventure of living counter-cultural and cross-cultural. I've not done well simply living with the status quo, always doing what is expected. Even at the youthful age of 80 that distant forlorn train whistle beacons my imagination. What is around the next bend? Will the bridge over that chasm still be intact?

A materialist worldview is not consciously comfortable with the notion of mystery. Yet it seems to me that much of life is surrounded by mystery, even the mundane things we do most everyday. Waiting for a "walk" signal to cross a busy street in a pedestrian lane requires mystery and faith. Can you be sure the traffic will stop? Yet I see Millennials enter that pedestrian at University and Euclid, their eyes fastened on their mobile, reading or sending a text, oblivious of the cars waiting just feet away. Some of those students might be on their way to a class in which the professor may well rant against belief in God as naïve and even morally wrong because of the ethic espoused by those who trust in a god. At the same time that professor might in a condescending manner speak tolerantly about other religions that may or may not be represented in that same classroom.

The same culture that touts consistency of life with regard to the environment and science is comfortable with inconsistency in the mundane of life and accepts that as normal. I call it mystery. Much in the same vein as accepting the reality of the spirit world in religions such as Shinto, Theravadic Buddhism and animisms. I think that same professor who ridicules Christianity would not ridicule the other religions. To be honest his ridicule is controlled more by political correctness than by any deep knowledge of the religions he endorses.

I think I'm more inclined toward mystery for two reasons. First I experienced the reality of the spirit world in Tantric Buddhism in Thailand. At first my Western worldview was the filter through which

I interpreted what I saw and experienced in spite of my training in cultural anthropology and intercultural studies.

Like other westerners I assumed that the amulets that hung from taxicab and bus rear view mirrors were simply ornamental. Then I talked one day to a Thai Taxi driver who had just come from the Buddhist temple. He proudly and reverently hung the amulet over his rear view mirror and then *waied*[33]. Like most Thai people he was friendly. I commented how attractive I thought it looked among the fragrant string of jasmine flowers that hung there too. He smiled and nodded. I asked him what was the meaning of the amulet. He said it was protection from accidents and then explained that the amulet had been blessed at the temple, where he purchased it. I asked how it would protect him. Rather embarrassed he explained that there are bad spirits (*phi*) that caused trouble and that his amulet would protect him from them and from accidents that might happen from bad drivers.

Though Thai people espoused Theravada Buddhism I realized that they lived by animistic beliefs.[34] Even the concept of deity[35] is held as relevant to both educated and less-educated people as core to the Thai worldview. The reason for this description of Thai phenomenology is to assert the centrality of the reality of the supernatural to this culture we lived among for a decade. Some of my colleagues lived as if all of this was superstition, asserting Western worldview assumptions about the reality of the *phi*. By contrast I accepted the reality of animistic worldview assumptions without endorsing those beliefs.

---

[33] The *wai* is a Thai form of respect and is used in greetings, apologies and religious events. The hands are placed together just under the nose with a slight nod of the head.

[34] Animism is the belief that both benevolent and malevolent spirits exist and are involved with human affairs and are capable of helping or harming human beings.

[35] *Prajao Yu Hua; i.e. God as Higher Intelligence in the Universe.*

Instead I looked for appropriate functional substitute forms that contained similar meaning in the indigenous culture.

My point is that the supernatural is indigenous to most cultures, even those that are westernizing. I'm led to believe that secularization that eliminates the supernatural is really a minority aberration among worldviews. Having lived in Japan, Thailand, and Philippines for protracted periods of time I've learned to adjust my Western worldview assumptions to respect those that contrast to my own.

So, what does all this mean? What advice do I give my millennial friends? Be slow to endorse a secularized Worldview that eliminates the supernatural. That would include God as personal, benevolent, involved, loving and good. Be cautious to accept uncritically the notion that the material is all that matters. Most worldviews are either conversant with or accept the reality of the metaphysical, the supernatural. We are in good company when we share that worldview in relevant ways in which God as one we can trust and love is the goal.

Perhaps this poem will say it better. Its something I wrote shortly after the questions I had about God were satisfied. When I arrived at peace living with mystery.

God & Philosophy

God! A word so large, yet small;
It's meaning lost in verbosity.
To some an idea so very droll,
Irrelevant religiosity.

To some, God is not.
He, or she, is dead; or never was.

While others, he can't be got.
Like grasping fuzz.

To a few, a precious lot,
There's naught to fear,
He can be got,
He's here and near!

A man once said, "I think, therefore I am."
And everyone replied, "This is great philosophy."
I suppose one could also say, "I think not, therefore I am not."
And make as much sense, theoretically.

Preachers? Teachers? Philosophers opinions?
Who's to say what is good philosophy?
These and more are sometimes the Devil's minions.
Creating confusion, Fog, arrogant hypocrisy.

Yet, from this fog, Reality can emerge;
Surprising Truth dispel
Anxious thoughts and ideas purge,
Faith propels.

For me, lets say I'm just a simple thinker,
Not given to profundity.
Still, if I don't' understand; with thoughts I cannot tinker,
Then is thought not mere Profanity?

Not from this well of incomprehensibility
Do I choose to drink!
A nobler Source, with more common feasibility
Is Whom I choose; I think.

Instead of human wisdom, He offered amazing grace,
I followed Him; He took me to a cross,
Where my soul I laid bare
He stripped away the dross.

Now, do I think less?
Leave my mind blank?
No! I'm happy to confess
I think more! To be frank!

CONCLUSION

Be a child of the light.

Someone asked me once for a list of books that were significant to my growth and development. One of them is Reinhold Niebuhr's *Children of Light, Children of Darkness.*[36] That book came into my life when I was in the midst of writing my dissertation *Dynamic Biblical Christianity in the Buddhist-Marxist Context.*[37] My purpose in doing that research was to examine how a Christian could live in the context of an impending Marxist culture in Northeast Thailand in the 1970's. It was expected then that the Marxist expansion from Vietnam through Cambodia and Laos would continue making Thailand the last Domino to fall in Southeast Asian sub continent.

I thought Niebuhr was especially relevant to my project. He was tenacious in his search for truth from a Biblical perspective and from within actual existing human political and social institutions He did not hold a static unchanging philosophy of political ethics. He grew from a pacifist socialist political position in the 1920's through stages to become the chief apologist for the Democratic Party's advocacy against Communism in the 1980's. He was not one to commit to

---

[36] *The Children of Light and the Children of Darkness*: A Vindication of Democracy and a Critique of Its Traditional Defense, **Reinhold Niebuhr**

[37] See *Dynamic Biblical Christianity in the Buddhist/Marxist Context of Northeast Thailand*, University Microfilms, Ann Arbor, Michigan. 1984.

only one idea regardless of changing times. I liked that because like culture; he was dynamic and able to change with changing times.

The idea of children of the light/darkness was not his idea. He got it from the Apostle Paul's admonition to the Christians living in the province of Thessalonica, modern day city of the same name in Greece.

> *1Now concerning the times and the seasons, brothers, " you have no need to have anything written to you. 2For you yourselves are fully aware that the day of the Lord will come like a thief in the night. 3While people are saying, "There is peace and security," then sudden destruction will come upon them as labor pains come upon a pregnant woman, and they will not escape. 4But you are not in darkness, brothers, for that day to surprise you like a thief. 5For you are all children of light, children of the day.*[38]

At times I feel as if I'm living in the days of darkness. Where I live is hopelessly polarized between angry so-called Progressives and fearful equally angry Conservatives. Each is convinced the other is the enemy, devoid of reasoning power and either uneducated or where the ohter has been reeducated in revisionist institutions. People judge each other as having minimal intellect based on hash-tags.

For example I was talking with a neighbor in my front yard when he looked at the sign I had planted there indicating whom I was voting for as president. His response was, "its people like you that cause all the problems." I was speechless. I couldn't believe that my value as a human being, one who was also a teacher by profession, would be assessed on the basis of which political party I was voting for. I'm sad to say it hasn't changed. In fact he's put a bumper sticker on his car that reads, "Unite Separately."

---

[38] I Thessalonians 5:1-8

There's lots of darkness in this world of all kinds. There is the darkness of crime in its many shapes and forms; breaking and entering to take what does not belong to the thief; taking the life someone either intentionally by murder or unintentionally by drunk driving; embezzling funds that belong to seniors; lying to hide up one's infidelity. The list is endless, all deeds of the darkness. Are these simply acts to be controlled somehow by external forces? Perhaps denying weapons would help control the forces of darkness?

Niebuhr said that darkness is essentially the practice of self-interest. Fulfilling selfish impulses is that which characterizes the children of Darkness. The children of light by contrast are characterized by selflessness, a kind of naïveté. They are citizens of what Jesus describes as the Kingdom of God, or Kingdom of Heaven. Unlike the children of darkness the children of light are open, believing, accepting and easily taken advantage of because of their child like honest and integrity. Niebuhr describes them as those who willingly, voluntarily lose the advantage because of their innocence.

The supreme example of course is Jesus before Pilate, when He refused to answer Pilate's questions but stood silently before him. Finally Pilate in exasperation said, *"You will not speak to me? Do you not know that I have authority to release you and authority to crucify you?"* The mood of the text indicates a calmer and less arrogant response from Jesus: *"You would have no authority over me at all unless it had been given you from above. Therefore he who delivered me over to you has the greater sin."*[39] I have a gut feeling these words infuriated Pilate. And yet they seem so characteristic of a naïve person who either does not care or is unaware of the effect His words have on one who cares a great deal about what people think.

---

[39] John 19:1-11 ESV

Remember Andre Trochme? I mentioned him earlier as an example of a risk taker, one who lived on the edge. He and his wife Magda pastored a Huguenot church in the village of Le Chambon in Southern France during those terrible years of WW II, 1939 to 1945. Both he and his wife were living examples of Kingdom citizens of the light during a very bleak period of human darkness.

Jews were being rounded up and sent to Concentration Camps by Hitler's Gestapo. Some managed to flee like frightened lambs pursued by ravenous wolves. Pastor Trochme and Magda fearlessly took those in who made their flight to their small village. When an obvious Jewish refugee appeared at their door seeking refuge Magda replied innocently and without drama "of course, of course, come in, come in." Without regard to her personal safety or that of her husband and children she invited them, fed and clothed them and then hid them. Some thought of Pastor Trochme and his wife as naive and foolish and I suppose they were naïve but they were not foolish. They were children of the Light.

On one occasion Jesus sent his disciples on an extensive what might be called evangelistic trip. In preparing them He said, *Behold, I am sending you out as sheep in the midst of wolves, so be ᴸwise as serpents and ᵍinnocent as doves.*[40]

The instruction to them was that they be far from foolish. Rather they were to be harmless, like a dove, defenseless in that sense. Much like Peter who had been told to bring a zealots sword to the Garden and then told to put it away when it was obviously the time to use it. At the same time they were to be wise as a snake. Snakes didn't have the best reputation. They are a metaphor for being wily, seductive and manipulative. Why did Jesus use that metaphor? I suppose the craftiness of the snake is a valuable defensive characteristic. Perhaps

---

[40] John 10:16-20 ESV

acting in what might appear to be foolish, naïve can be considered an evasive gesture that masks the real intent.

An older woman cleaned the church at Le Chambon. Among her responsibilities was to raise the flag each morning and take it down in the evening. With the invasion of the Germans into France she was required to fly the German flag. She was told by the German commandant that she must raise the German flag and not the French flag, which she did. However, one day the German commandant observed the German flag flying upside down. Furious the commandant rebuked her to which she replied that she was just a simple woman. Time and again the darkness of the German occupation was frustrated by the naïveté of the otherwise defenseless children of the light. Eberhard Bethge, biographer of Dietrich Bonheoffer, pointed out that there was a point at which violent resistance to Hitler's Third Reich not possible. It was at that point when the metaphor of wise as serpent and harmless as dove was its most relevant.

Adam and Eve in their Pre-fall state were children of the light. They knew no sin, had not yet eaten the forbidden fruit and were living in innocent obedience to their creator. The text doesn't say it but I think they were naïve. That snake of the garden deceived them without a lot of effort. She took and ate without coercion and they justly experienced the consequences of their actions. Then God comes calling. I suspect He knew all along where they were hiding but He calls them out anyway, I think it's God's way of encouraging repentance. They emerge, admit their failure, repentance it's called; and in that moment they begin the long painful journey back to their pre-fall state of innocence as children of the light. I believe that's who we are; children of the light. What's left is to continue the journey in faith and embracing with joy and anticipation of the risks. I recommend it.

Printed in the United States
By Bookmasters